THE NATION'S CHILDREN

in three volumes

THE NATION'S CHILDREN

Edited by Eli Ginzberg

3: PROBLEMS AND PROSPECTS

Published 1 9 6 0 for the Golden Anniversary
White House Conference on Children and Youth
by COLUMBIA UNIVERSITY PRESS, NEW YORK

GOLDEN ANNIVERSARY
WHITE HOUSE CONFERENCE ON
CHILDREN AND YOUTH

HONORARY CHAIRMAN
The President of the United States
Dwight D. Eisenhower

HONORARY VICE CHAIRMAN
The Secretary of Health, Education, and Welfare
Arthur S. Flemming

CHAIRMAN
Mrs. Rollin Brown

VICE CHAIRMEN

Hurst R. Anderson
Philip S. Barba, M.D.
Mrs. James E. Blue
Robert E. Bondy
Erwin D. Canham
Donald K. David
Luther Foster
Msgr. Raymond J. Gallagher

Mrs. Frank Gannett
Edward D. Greenwood, M.D.
Daryl P. Harvey, M.D.
Donald S. Howard
Ruth A. Stout
Rabbi Marc H. Tanenbaum
Rev. Dr. William J. Villaume

SECRETARY
Mrs. Katherine B. Oettinger

ASSOCIATE DIRECTOR
Isabella J. Jones

EXECUTIVE DIRECTOR
Ephraim R. Gomberg

COMMITTEE ON STUDIES
Chairman: Eli Ginzberg *

Leona Baumgartner, M.D.
Mrs. Fitzhugh W. Boggs
Mrs. Wright W. Brooks
Sister Mary de Lourdes *
Jack R. Ewalt, M.D.
Mrs. Otto L. Falk
Mrs. David Graham
Margaret Hickey
Reuben L. Hill, Jr.*
A. John Holden
Rt. Rev. Arthur Carl
 Lichtenberger

Harry M. Lindquist
Mrs. Alvin A. Morrison
Captain Frank J. Popello
William L. Pressly
Milton J. E. Senn, M.D.*
Joseph Stokes, M.D.*
Ruth A. Stout *
Rabbi Marc H. Tanenbaum *
John Tannehill
Ralph W. Tyler *
Whitney M. Young, Jr.*

* Member of the Steering Committee.

CONTENTS

INTRODUCTION

by ELI GINZBERG

SOMEWHERE there may be a society where change is so slow that it cannot be observed, where there are neither general problems nor specific prospects. Such a society may be afflicted, and frequently is, by immediate scourges natural and man-made, but it may simply accept misfortune.

How different it is in our own society. We are always beset by problems and as soon as we solve one, two new ones take its place. This is true of our expectations: as soon as one objective is taken, we set ourselves two others. To paraphrase Samuel Gompers, the American people always want more.

The more dynamic a society is, the more it is likely to be beset by problems, for with change comes disturbance. But the more affluent a society is, the greater are its opportunities to solve the problems which change creates.

The third volume of *The Nation's Children*, as its title indicates, is focused on this point-counterpoint of "Problems

Eli Ginzberg is Director of the Conservation of Human Resources Project, Director of Staff Studies of the National Manpower Council, and Professor of Economics at Columbia University.

and Prospects." Among the problem groups singled out are rural youth, youth in minority groups, and youth in trouble with the law. These are important both because of the large numbers involved and because of the difficulties our society has experienced in handling their problems.

The volume also presents reviews of the voluntary and government mechanisms available to mitigate social mal-functioning and the extent to which we make use of these mechanisms. Finally, there are several contributions that assess the potential for adjustment in our basic institutions; we must control change if we are not to be overwhelmed by it.

In studying rural youth, Professor Kolb calls attention to the continuing large-scale migration from rural areas into urban communities and the difficulties that the migrants face as they seek to orient themselves to a new way of life and to new occupations, difficulties that are accentuated be-cause so many of these youth have had an inferior education. Further, Professor Kolb indicates that those who remain be-hind must adapt themselves to "agribusiness," unless they belong to submerged farm families who do not even have the chance to adapt. Farm communities are further handi-capped because they have lost their former cohesion and are increasingly buffeted by decisions made by leadership groups located in distant centers of power.

In his delineation of the major factors influencing Negro youth in the South, Dr. Lewis Jones emphasizes the order of change that has taken place during the past two decades on every front—legal, educational, and economic. He reminds us that segregation is a system of deliberate and systematic exploitation, a system that denies the Negro his basic civil rights as well as access to good schools and good jobs. Fortunately this oppressive system is crumbling and Negro youth are increasingly in the foreground of the struggle. Dr. Jones warns that some of these youth are so unsettled by the gap between their inalienable rights and the continuing exploitation and repression to which they are still subjected, that they sometimes respond in ways that cannot lead to constructive results. But in general he has a more favorable reading of the trend. While the Southern farm has little to offer Negro youth, many of them will seek the realization of their hopes and dreams in the urban centers of the South convinced that the rabid segregationists are a diminishing minority.

A prevalent assumption in the United States is that we have but a single minority problem—the Negro. And quantitatively, this is so. But in the Southwest, in California and Colorado, as well as in New York City, there is another significant minority, the Spanish-speaking people—the Spanish Americans, Mexican Americans, and Puerto Ricans, who, according to Professor Burma, total about 3.5 million.

Although the Spanish Americans have been in the United States for ten generations, most of the other Spanish-speaking groups have only recently immigrated and therefore face many of the problems that bedevil newcomers; since they are less well-educated and less well-trained than the native population, they find themselves at the bottom of the social-economic ladder. But, as Professor Burma says, the educational picture is constantly becoming brighter for these groups, and with better education goes better jobs and a greater opportunity for acculturation.

If one problem of American youth were to be singled out because of our overriding concern with it, it would unquestionably be juvenile delinquency. This evidence of serious social dislocation among large numbers of young people is a sharp reminder of our collective shortcomings as parents, neighbors, and citizens. Professor MacIver emphasizes that while the initial source of delinquent behavior must be sought within the family, the family in turn is much affected by the forces in its immediate environment and the larger society. Low economic status, overcrowded housing, lack of training and experience for competitive urban life, and social discrimination tend to be characteristic of high-delinquency areas. And Professor MacIver places particular stress on the vulnerability of newcomers to the city who must face the most difficult problems with the least equipment. Professor MacIver discusses the importance of preventive and rehabilitative measures aimed at eradicating as rapidly as possible the pathological conditions conducive to the growth of delinquency and at providing additional resources in the form of facilities and personnel to help reverse the antisocial behavior of young people before it becomes fixed.

This cursory review should have made at least one point clear: that there are many children and youth in the United States who continue to require special help. But large as these special groups are, they by no means include all children and youth in need of help.

Elizabeth Wickenden in her essay on voluntary welfare services and Eveline Burns in her review of the government's role in child and family welfare assess the scope and adequacy of our social effort on behalf of children whose families are unable to provide for them.

Miss Wickenden calls attention to the strength of the American tradition of reliance on mutual aid and the important innovations which voluntary organizations have to their credit. The extent of present-day voluntary efforts is suggested by the finding that $400 million was raised by community chests during 1959 for 27,000 separate agencies in 2,000 American communities. Miss Wickenden points out that, while many families still experience economic hardship, the heart of the voluntary effort is being directed toward the prevention or alleviation of problems reflecting social disequilibrium. The more voluntary agencies contribute to the reduction of divorce, desertion, illegitimacy, delinquency, and mental illness, the greater will be their contribution to the well-being of children who are the principal victims of these social ills.

Professor Burns describes the tremendous part that government now plays in providing assistance to those in need; she then cites major shortcomings that still persist in this elaborate structure of public aid. Among the weak programs is the Aid to Dependent Children's Program which, in Professor Burns' opinion, has no clearly defined policy and which fails to provide an adequate level of support for those whom it purports to help. Professor Burns further points out that despite the acknowledged desirability of keeping children in

their own homes, 70 percent of all public resources for children is still spent on foster care. More needs to be done to
assist working mothers, low-income families, and children
of broken homes. Professor Burns concludes her review with
the hope that the American people will more adequately
honor their expressed concern for the welfare of children
and youth.

Dean Henry David's paper, covering the triple subject of
"work, women, and children," provides a transition from the
more specific problem areas and the social mechanisms available to cope with them to transformations in the larger society that affect the population as a whole. The focus of his
concern is the rapid rise in the employment of women outside the home, especially married women, which has been
proceeding in recent decades so rapidly that it might appropriately be called a social revolution.

Dr. David indicates that no single factor can account for
this "revolution" which is connected not only with the needs
of the economy but also with significant changes affecting
women, including an increase in their marriage rate, a lower-
ing of their average age of marriage, the earlier completion of
their families, and an increase in their life expectancy. But
it is strange that, in a child-centered culture such as ours, this
revolution which impinges so directly on the child, has not
been seriously studied. Dr. David concludes that such a study
could not fail to provide a new range of understanding of
the nation's recent social and economic history.

The remaining three essays in the volume by Nelson
Foote, Eric Larrabee, and Norman Cousins are contributions

of another dimension. These authors raise questions about the inner springs of American society and of the contemporary world and speculate about our present position and about what the future holds in store for us.

Dr. Foote reminds us that each generation sets its own aspirations and goals. There is no certainty of greater control over society as time proceeds; all that is certain is greater control over nature. Looking back over this century, Dr. Foote is impressed with the sharp changes in the stance of successive generations; looking ahead, he raises what he believes may become the central issue for the present generation—how to adjust to peace if the wheel of fortune makes this turn.

In a peaceful world, self-realization must be sought as much through leisure activities as through work. But Dr. Foote suggests that a Puritan culture, however much the Puritanism has been diluted, will probably encounter difficulties in learning how to live with its good fortune.

The place of childhood in American culture is the concern of Eric Larrabee. He differentiates between the need of adults to be concerned with the nurturing of their successors and the special situation which prevails in the United States where so many adult tensions and frustrations are projected onto children. Mr. Larrabee reviews the changing styles in child-rearing, which he relates to the value structure in American life during the past half-century. He argues for a basic skepticism toward prevailing doctrines of child care and for caution, so that we do not become enslaved by another tyranny of our own making. He concludes with a plea to permit the new generation to develop their own worries, believing that a little inattention will do it (and the rest of us) a world of good!

The concluding essay in the present volume, as well as in the series, is Norman Cousins' thoughtful discussion of the human commonwealth. Mr. Cousins begins by recalling some simple but often neglected facts. He argues that the rate of change in the lives of nations and peoples has greatly accelerated during the last decade, much more than most of us realize, for we all suffer from lack of perspective. He further believes that since education must always be geared to the challenge of the times, there is an urgent need to reform our educational structure if we want to control and not be engulfed by the changes that are under way.

We must begin by de-provincializing education; both East and West belong to the same human commonwealth. We must recognize the basic unity of most religions. We must discard the stereotypes that hamstring the scholar and enflame the passions of the citizen. We must recognize the human situation for what it is and help the young to understand that all men must learn to live on one planet.

Young and old, East and West, the planet itself, cannot flourish or even survive unless the lesson of "the human commonwealth" is learned—and learned quickly.

THE NATION'S CHILDREN

3: PROBLEMS AND PROSPECTS

THE OLD GENERATION AND THE NEW

by NELSON N. FOOTE

THE WHITE HOUSE Conference on Children and Youth is a kind of periodic national audit of our long-term hopes for our children and their partial realization. It exceeds in perspective not only the annual reports by which we examine our progress in many other fields but also the decennial census which counts the various units of which the nation is constituted. Each decade it tries to formulate some sense of the kind of environment that would be more favorable than the current one for the kind of people that we want the rising generation to become.

To discuss the kind of environment that would favor the rising generation is to take a very special point of view. It is to generalize the roles of parent and of professional person who cares for children to the extent of considering the United States as a vast household, as if its citizens were universally interested in fostering the development of their offspring. No one who has gone through the agitation of a referendum on

Nelson N. Foote is Research Consultant, Sociology, for the General Electric Company.

a school bond issue would take that assumption for granted. Nonetheless, it is a useful standpoint from which to think about what would be possible if everyone would in fact play his role as citizen with the same seriousness as that of parent.

Aspirations and Reality

Each generation sets some bounds to what it deems possible, as well as declaring some goals. Certain bounds are fixed by nature, but others are only taken as given, and a later generation often makes up its mind to assault such limitations as unnecessary suppositions. It is often the differing assessments of what is possible and what is forbidden by circumstances beyond control by which one generation is distinguished from another. Parents may aspire to the same state of affairs as their children, but consider the risk of trying to attain it so great that they fear that their children too would only be hurt by the attempt. And sometimes they are right.

There is no certainty of progress from lesser to greater control over society as time proceeds. There is some advance in control of nature. One need not be very old to remember how uncertain life was before antibiotics, even for the young person who expects never to die. But the illusion that progress extends from the realm of technical control over natural processes to that of human relations, however stubbornly preached by self-persuaded social scientists, withers in the glare of recent history. Nuclear physics has raised the threat of total obliteration as its way of clarifying the issue. Some uncertainties of natural origin remain, like the weather, but on the whole, the kinds of restriction that arbitrarily limit how far we may develop are those we impose upon each other. And while these change from generation to generation, their obsolescence is illusory evidence on which to base a claim of progress.

Giving up the idea of progress is hard in practice even when granted intellectually, nourished as we are on the rhetoric of education and material advancement. Only last summer, for instance, I conversed in the Brussels airport with an Indian attorney from an Arabic country known for its oil riches. He told me of how justice is served in that area through the mutilation of offenders, foreigners of course exempted. I asked him what became of the victims other than those who are beheaded, and he replied that the ruler permits their hospitalization by Christian missionaries. He succeeded in briefly reviving my childhood sense that I was fortunate to enjoy citizenship in an advanced civilization. Such a sense, however, cannot survive a trip through the nearest veterans' hospital. Human beings are no less capable here than elsewhere, now than before, of treating each other horribly. I shall only mention a file I used to keep of the crimes of parents against children.

When we experience a sense of movement from worse to better in our relations with each other, it is like the movement toward the climax of a play, rather than like the steady improvements in the properties of steel over the past century. In real life, unlike the drama, each plot leads into another, but there is no necessary cumulation of happiness for the actors. The next series of events is always in jeopardy of passing from better to worse.

In facing equally this constant jeopardy of fortune, there is justice among the generations, between one generation and the next. Save in relative control of nature, which will always remain incomplete, it is as good or bad to be born one time as another. How we acquit ourselves in our own time cannot be attributed to our choice of parents, but only to how we utilize the time we have. And likewise, when we assume the role of parents, we cannot guarantee success to our children. However lavishly we set the stage for them, the stage may further but cannot control the plot or its outcome. Indeed, if we assume that our children want what we want as the outcome of their existence, and bend every resource to getting it for them, we can do them the greatest disservice, since they would not recognize the outcome as truly theirs, nor would the striving to achieve it be theirs.

What does it mean, then, to aim during the next decade toward the provision of an environment favorable to children and youth? If each lived in a world of his own making, and could work out his own fate individually, there would be no logical sense to this venture in prophecy. But for good or evil, our destinies are intertwined, across as within generations. We act in each other's plots, and while in real life there is no omniscient author as in the drama, we not only set the stage but continually cast each other in the parts we play.

Unraveling the complications of the fact that parents are particularly potent in casting their children into the roles they perform—with some assistance from professional teachers and employers—is thus no easy task. Because of the narrative concreteness of each generation's span of events, it may be helpful to look closely at recent developments before attempting further to generalize philosophically.

To this point we have argued only that each generation has its own peculiar plot to fulfill, in roles and setting which have been cast by its predecessors, but the evolution of which can neither be dictated nor guaranteed by them. There is not even a way for one generation to sacrifice itself by denying its own obligation to realize the possibilities of its own time. When this viewpoint is applied to events of the decades traversed by the White House Conference on Children and Youth, what does it portend for the next ten years?

The first of these conferences was held in 1909 at the behest of President Theodore Roosevelt. His name is reminiscent of the period during which the United States emerged from preoccupation with its own westward settlement and inferiority to Europe, and began to take pride in its own distinctive contributions to world civilization. The Great White Fleet which circled the globe and the completion of the Panama Canal climaxed this new portrayal of the country abroad. Meanwhile the several cross-currents of the election of 1912 manifested at home the desires of all segments of the population to share in the sense of having completed the building of a nation.

The next White House Conference came after victory in the war had been celebrated, the great steel strike had been lost, and the country had been increasingly transformed from being an agricultural to being an industrial nation. Except for the dethroned farmers whose wheat had been so mighty in winning the war, most people became oriented toward making money through manufacturing and commerce. With the rise of the automobile, the small town which had set the pattern for rural America was overthrown by the city. The emphasis of the forthcoming 1920s was to be on the relaxation of restriction and inhibition, on self-assertion and success.

There is no reason to expect historical events to fall neatly into decennial intervals, and they do not. On the other hand, from the viewpoint of parent and child generations, there is some grouping of events around major turning points, which sometimes occur that close together. From Armistice Day in 1918 until the beginning of the depression was not quite eleven years, and World War II began in September of 1939 with the invasion of Poland by the Nazis.

What Defines a Generation?

The traditional conception of a generation in time was thirty years, about the average period from a male's birth until the birth of his first male child. Nowadays a generation so defined is much closer to twenty years in duration, due to earlier marriage, smaller gap in age of husband and wife, and less emphasis on male children. From the beginning of this century, therefore, we may speak of either two or three generations having elapsed, speaking chronologically, with 1930 as the dividing year in the former case, 1920 and 1940 in the latter. And in either case, 1960 becomes another, if somewhat less dramatic, turning point between this generation and the next.

The turning points between generations are more sociological than chronological, despite intriguing coincidences with historical intervals. What distinguishes one generation from another is not a sequence of small gradations but rather marked qualitative divergences, occurring rather suddenly. Certain historical events usually act as watersheds, causing the thinking of those who come to adulthood before these events to flow into more or less parallel channels, whereas the orientations of those who come to adulthood afterward, while likewise conforming with their contemporaries, flow in very different directions from the thinking of their predecessors. Thus World War I, the depression and World War II have been the major turning points for American young people of this century. As of this moment, the nature of a new crisis differentiating the pre-1960 generation from the post-1960 generation is not evident, but it is imaginable. Hitherto the major turning points have regularly been provided by drastic shifts in either international relations or domestic economy or both simultaneously. Since international politics and domestic economies constitute the principal structures with which young people grow up and adults pursue their careers, it is imaginable that they will likewise be the basis for the next turning point in the formation of the new generation from the present cohorts of children and youth. Indeed, in retrospect a few years from now, we may wonder why it was not obvious to us at this moment that a great crisis in our society would be constituted by a substantial increment in confidence in the duration of peace.

If Prime Minister Khrushchev were to succeed in making the kinds of guarantees to Americans which would give them some confidence in the peaceable intentions of Soviet Russia, a considerable economic crisis would probably result. Without indulging in further speculation as to the likelihood of this being the turning point which differentiates the 1960s, and far less stating it as a definite prediction, let us at least recognize this possibility. It does provide an example of the kind of turning point which would compare in universal influence with the previous turning points of this century.

The peculiar mechanism by which generations are differentiated is thus simultaneously historical and biographical. The historical events which produce the watersheds are economic and political shifts which affect the present and prospective conditions of life of all persons coming to adulthood when they occur. That is, they cause each young person's estimate of what is possible for him to differ from the estimate made by his parents at that same phase in their own life histories. Biographically, membership in a distinctive generation is not so much the result of when one is born as when he becomes an adult, an event far less definitely placed chronologically and one which can be quite substantially hastened or postponed by historical events. Some boys have found themselves in combat overseas before they were out of their teens, just as many girls are now finding themselves mothers before twenty. On the other hand, in pursuing certain professions requiring advanced training, the dependency of young people on their parents is frequently prolonged through most of their twenties. The transition from adolescence into adulthood, therefore, is to be identified realistically primarily by the making of those major commitments which tend to

structure the remainder of one's life history—choice of voca-
tion, choice of mate, and choice of friends and models of
behavior. These major life-determining decisions tend to in-
terlock; their intercontingency adds to their stability.

As the principal mechanism for differentiating historical
generations, the biographical mechanism of making basic
career choices may seem peculiar to a free society, where
individuals are encouraged to make them with minimum reliance on parental recommendation. Certainly much attention is concentrated on vocational and marital selection in
the United States, where it is widely believed that only voluntary commitments can be counted sound. It could be argued,
however, that the same mechanism operates even in societies
where parents are seemingly more authoritative in determining their children's life-plans. Most significantly, few societies
remain in which the control of one generation extends to its
grandchildren. And thus, even where children do not themselves openly resist parental direction, a way remains by
which vast concerted changes can occur from one generation
to the next.

Each generation, apart from planning its own course during adulthood, resolves to raise its children in various ways
differently from the way in which it was raised by its parents.
Many men and women who grew up as only children during
the 1920s and '30s, for example, resolved that their children
would not be only children, but would grow up with brothers
and sisters. It is quite true that each generation also takes
for granted that many of the ways of its parents were right,
and transmits them unquestioningly and almost unwittingly

to its children. Thus the scheme of generations may be said to provide naturally for both continuity and change, and it would be unrealistic to emphasize either to the exclusion of the other.

In the same manner, the coming together of a man and woman in marriage produces a domestic environment for their offspring which is likely to be different in important ways from that in which either grew up. This mixing of backgrounds through marriage increases the chance of novel outcomes, viewed from the standpoint of individual biography. From the statistical standpoint, however, it also tends toward the diffusion and assimilation of the various strains of family culture, so that cumulatively children may differ more from their predecessors than from their contemporaries.

Finally, in devoting detail to the mechanism by which intergenerational distinctions evolve, it must be noted that the various generations, as groups of actors in society, overlap in time and thus interact. It has become well recognized that the outlooks of adolescents are heavily shaped by their peers. The individual makes chums of others who are crossing the same thresholds of development, pondering the same difficult questions of belief and self-evaluation. He does not entirely think for himself, however great his insistence on independence from parental guidance, but represents the combined thinking of those members of his own generation with whom he is in intimate contact. And of course the web of such communication among age-mates is not compartmentalized within particular segments or strata of communities, but seems to spread in an unbroken web across the land, and

even into other lands. Through challenge and debate, vague
alterations of emphasis in values often lead not to resolution
of differences and harmony, but to sharpening and polariza-
tion of views, to the crystallization of contrasts, and even to
conflict between adjoining generations. One may cite as a
familiar example the conscientious mutual disapproval of the
ethics of financial management practiced by parents reared
during the depression and children reared during the continuously upgrading prosperity since.

The New Generation

Returning then to our example of the possibility of peace as
a major turning point in the planning of life-careers by the
new generation, it is all too obvious that here is an assumption as unprovable as it is controversial, one that could readily
polarize the population along generational lines, needlessly
perhaps but effectively. It is not so long ago that it took the
most brutal of facts to convince the majority of Americans
that involvement in war was unavoidable. Yet a scant twenty
years later, it will be equally hard for the majority to become
confident that a long period of peace is possible.

Yet peace is possible, peace in the reality of a confidence
sufficient to permit substantial disarmament. If peace in the
world were to endure for even another twenty years, it could
be argued, it would be for the first time in the history of the
world that potential combatants, industriously equipping
themselves to the ultimate in arms, have not used them. Yet
every day we are confronted with events that are happening
for the first time in the history of mankind. Many young

people are so accustomed to the surpassing of previous limitations on technological prowess that they scoff at any who
doubt the eventual success of the latest space-traveling pipe-
dream as very old-fashioned indeed.

Of course, to achieve right relations among blocks of humanity is not a similar technical problem, as we have made
plain from the outset. And just how it is to be done is
exactly the major challenge confronting the present generation, beside which the perfection of lunar rockets is a beg-
ging of the question. The kind of training for the one is
utterly different from that which has the best chance of
achieving the other, and over the appropriate training for
youth the conflict between the generations will probably
wax hotter. Indeed, on the axiom that the dominant theme
of a period always seems in retrospect as if it ought to have
been obvious to participants at the time, the plausibility of
our hypothetical suggestion that the exchange of visits between president and prime minister might prove to be the
turning point between the last and the next generation becomes uncomfortably persuasive.

For the sake of perspective, let us step back a moment to
the late 1940s, when clearly a new generation was emerging.
Following the success of the Marshall Plan in averting Communism in Europe through promoting economic recovery,
President Truman set forth his bold, new program for extending the principle to the underdeveloped nations. His
Point Four Program seemed to this writer then, and still
seems today, an ideal vehicle for mobilizing the technical
talent of the young people of this nation for accomplishing

the nontechnical objective of establishing a just world society, one that would extend the sway of our favored values
without encroaching on the autonomy of other people. It
might have given expression not only to the vastly more
cosmopolitan public opinion that emerged from the experiences of World War II, without diminishing the emphasis
on economic achievement that distinguishes us as a people.
I was wrong, as was President Truman, in appraising the
temper of the people. He was far more right in recognizing
soon after that the majority of the citizenry of 1948 still had
memories of the depression which dominated their thoughts
about the future. It may be that his mistake in judgment
or timing was only in not treating public opinion about international relations as consistent with opinion regarding the
domestic economy. And if this were the error, it need not be
repeated, at least in dealing with our more-or-less hypothetical example. In a sense, events have given to the American
public a second chance to consider grand strategy with regard
to domestic economy and world politics, and to members of
the new generation the chance to design their lives by a
different set of assumed limitations and possibilities.

The terms of the overall equation by which people calcu-
late the outcomes to be expected from moving in various
directions are different from what they were in 1948 in only a
few essentials, but the balance of numbers between the old
and the new generation is much changed, and the decision
may well be opposite. In 1948, it may be remembered, unemployment in engineering and related professions was high,
and college students were being dissuaded from entering

these pursuits. Now, of course, the most common plaint is that enrollments in technical schools, already at a stupendous peak, are far below requirements, if we are to man the advanced facilities that are being constructed to match Communist or commercial competition. Secondly, instead of the economic uncertainty of that year, we have bounded briskly out of a brief recession, and foresee output climbing so vigorously that hampering effects of the steel strike are disregarded. And finally, while the aggressive competition of the Soviet Union for influence among the uncommitted nations is far more visible, the neutrals appear more ready to declare their allegiance. What we seem to have, in other words, is a clarification of a situation that may have been imminent in 1948—even with Korea included among the evidence—that what impends is not a conflict but a peaceful competition. If this interpretation is made by the younger generation of the world with which they are confronted, that the only kind of peace that is possible with the Soviet Union is an indefinite period of strenuous competition, it may seem preferable to indefinite waiting for the first missile to arrive. Certainly on the other side, Russian young people seem powerfully tempted by civilian goods and services, so tempted that they may be willing to rest their hopes for global eminence on their prowess in economic and scientific competition.

If the 1960s become a period of strenuous competition with the Soviet Union, this will be quite different from most of the 1950s, which were largely occupied with holding the Communists in check abroad while devoting resources at home primarily to upgrading the physical standard of living, to achieving affluence, as the phrase has caught it. Merely to hold back the Communists abroad and to increase the level of consumption at home are not the kind of national or societal purposes which translate readily into individual life plans, as they are almost nondirective in their implications. It is not surprising that people during this immediate period, especially those reaching adulthood, have been perturbed by the question of who they are and what they want to become —the question of identity.

In choosing as its most influential guiding document Erik Erikson's *Childhood and Society*, the White House Conference on Children and Youth in 1950 chose prophetically. Erikson's book was a penetrating formulation of the task of finding identity when restrictions on the individual's choice among alternatives are removed. Before the coming of the affluent society, it always seemed to make sense to uphold as ideal a society in which everyone could achieve the fullest expression of all his potentialities. That slogan has now become obsolete, as the surplus of possible courses of development and the absence of restrictions force one to set his own limits, choose the few paths to which he will voluntarily confine himself, if he is not to be a futile dilettante. The past ten years have taught people, especially the younger ones making their lifetime choices, to view more tolerantly those conditions of life which remain fixed, to accept as valuable the idea of permanent commitments, which can liberate more energies and personal resources than the defunct state of remaining uncommitted. The corollary of the problem posed by Erickson, that serious commitment, voluntary but nonrevocable, is a positive good, has only slowly emerged. It is in a sense the legacy of the 1950s to the '60s, which now offer the opportunity to the new generation to build upon it as a positive premise.

Self-Realization, Fun, and Morality

As we look into the '60s from this biographical premise that serious commitments are good, and from the historical premise that we can enjoy peace if we are willing to undergo strenuous competition with the Soviet Union, various further implications and corollaries of these premises can be foreseen emerging during the next decade or two. Perhaps a useful point from which to start in laying these out is to go back to another book which most aptly foretold the concern of people becoming adults during the '50s, David Riesman's *The Lonely Crowd.* Near its close, Professor Riesman suggests that, since so many people do not find self-realization in their work, the widespread growth of leisure might make it possible for them to cultivate their autonomy in play.

Even at the time of his statement of this proposition, Riesman was open to criticism for surrendering so readily the occupational realm as a sphere for autonomous self-development, for the establishment of identity. But he saw self-realization in work the privilege of only a small percentage of our population, and from the standpoint of the year in which he wrote—a year when engineers were often unemployed—he expected that percentage to dwindle. But throughout the succeeding period, the most rapid growth in the labor force has been precisely in those occupations which offer their participants a professional career. And autonomy and identity through work are close to synonymous with those kinds of occupations which can be called careers. The extent and speed of professionalization during the succeeding years has been prodigious, yet seems minor in relation to what is coming. Of this, the currently over-three-million enrollment in higher education gives only a hint. The vast rise in industrial research and development, civilian as much as military, seems likewise on the lower part of an exponential curve. And so with the rise of all kinds of professional services and institutions—medical, educational, and recreational.

In respect to leisure and recreation, David Riesman was even righter than he thought he was, because it is in the sphere of play that the new features of personal development have become most fully clarified, in the model of the advanced amateur. And it is here that the ambiguities of the relationships between work and play in personal development have become clarified, with boundless implications for society at large.

Adults play roles in society both as producers and as consumers. It is more revealing to describe their styles of life in terms of producer and consumer roles than simply of work and play, especially when work connotes only gainful employment. It is primarily in respect to play—to self-chosen interests which occupy leisure—that people's roles as consumers can and do become differentiated. To the extent that consumption refers only to necessities—food, clothing, and shelter—consumption patterns tend to be differentiated mainly with respect to quantity, and thus reflect the differing incomes associated with the various producer roles. But as the discretionary portions of incomes rise—while in the aggregate real incomes become both higher and relatively more equal—the patterns of consumer expenditures of money, time, energy, and attention can and do become more and more representative of genuine family styles of life, less and less indicative merely of the earning power of the principal breadwinner of each household. Upgrading leads to differentiation. This differentiation is most visible in connection with leisure pursuits, and more visible still as these self-chosen interests are pursued more seriously.

Where for the multitude during recent decades, work has been set off sharply from play, for the serious amateur, the competence, application and creativity of his play can be distinguished from those of the skilled professional only by his not making a living therefrom. The degree of enjoyment, the voluntary commitment of long hours to learning and practice, the multiple forms of expression of serious interest —publications, associations, advanced courses, reading, thinking, meeting, trying new techniques, which are found among serious professionals, are also common to serious amateurs.

In this paradoxical combination of seriousness with voluntary commitment to group-developed standards of performance, the growth of leisure and the growth of professionalization since the war join to shape the main outline of our coming society. The early manifestations are everywhere, in camera clubs, boating magazines, specialized shops to handle equipment, adult education courses, and inservice training seminars. What the devotees of each special interest may not have noticed is how parallel the lines of development have been among the other specialties. Also, while the movement toward serious pursuits of self-chosen interests in work and play has gone far enough for recognition as a general movement, it has not as yet embraced more than a small minority. Most of the effort to realize in full the meaning of a leisured professional society still lies ahead, although very near ahead.

Unhappily, the signs of the times are not clear enough to be immune to misapprehension. Even though, for instance, the desire of the sons of factory workers to become engineers runs far ahead of existing facilities and enrollments some vocal critics of our educational system profess that not enough high-school students are being pressed into science and mathematics. Even though Dr. Conant has pointed out the vast waste of talent in the discouragement of achievement among girls, it continues along with the waste of skilled manpower already existing among minority groups. As reported by the President's Commission on Higher Education in 1948, a high percentage of the most able high-school students still do not go to college. There is no dearth of evidence as to the abundance of aspiration to professionalization. There is, however, little recognition of and reliance on the voluntary auspices under which the younger generation wishes to conduct its affairs, its insistence, to put the matter flatly, that *work be fun.* The older generation, or at least some of its presumed spokesmen, apparently do not grant that such a demand is legitimate; they cannot grasp that it is possible for the world's work to get done, or for the world's political crises to be met, on that basis.

Yet when fun is seen neither as an escape from work nor as a preparation for work, but as a feasible means of making any worthwhile activity a path to self-realization, it is plain that fun offers as sturdy and effective a moral discipline as work. Indeed, there is no difference, because the traditional discipline of work was not really the discipline of work but of a society which imposed unpleasant toil on the majority as a condition of consumption. Work was not chosen in most cases on its own account but as a means of making a living. "Just a job" was the typical way of speaking of it, but that is not how one describes a profession. A profession offers not just a job but a career, and its morality springs from the assumption that it was entered by voluntary commitment, that one is motivated to pursue it not primarily to make a living, which is taken for granted, but to receive the respect of his colleagues and more or less directly to serve those who need what one produces.

The concept of professional ethics is familiar, but the idea that fun imposes morality on behavior, while not new, remains still a rather strange notion to many. They are familiar with the rules of games, and know that without their observance, games cannot go on. Games evince a higher degree of interest among participants in observance of rules than occurs under any form of government. The only extension of the principle involved is that the rules of the game must apply more widely as the game itself is widened to include more and more of the world's work. The serious amateur, as he becomes involved with others in his interest, plays a game with very strict rules of honor. One often sees, for example, sportsmen who are far more punctilious about the conservation of wild life and the forests and streams than are those who utilize them merely for a livelihood. The etiquette and reciprocal sensitivity among members of voluntary associations are always superior to those found where relations are compulsory. The socializing effect of games on children has long been noted by child psychologists, but only recently has it become apparent that the same principle might operate in humanizing some of the less civilized features of adult life.

In previous times, when a society became oriented toward leisure and enjoyment, it was often to the neglect of work, which was imposed on some subject group, and of decent government. Now for the first time in history it begins to appear that this outcome does not have to be feared; indeed conducted as fun, both work and government are likely to be performed with stronger conscience and higher competence than under the pressures of duty and necessity. The beauty of such a revolution is that it requires no one to arm and assault an enemy; one has only to relax and enjoy it, to relax, that is, the anxieties which inhibit serious commitment to playful purposes, and the free flow of energies which follows.

Perhaps the ability of the older generation to accept this more playful way of life is greater than the voices of alarm among them suggest. Certainly the past generation has seen family life take on a more festive aspect, along with a keener and more responsible interest in the development of children, among fathers as well as mothers. As parenthood has become more of a hobby, it has also become more of a profession. As many have said, children have become consumption items, wanted for their own sake, and not as extra hands. Not so long ago big, strong boys were the favorite choices for adoption, where now requests for baby girls are the most frequent. Professor Jessie Bernard has pointed out that nowadays the position of the child in the home has become very much like the role of the guest. Similarly with regard to occupations outside the home: when one goes to conventions of people of almost any occupation, one finds mingled the festive with the serious aspect of the professional concept.

Nowadays most people live not only long enough to see their children develop into adulthood, but also their children's children. Their span of life thus may be said to cover three generations. As parents, with their own children, they get to re-live vicariously, but by direct observation, their own experiences of growing up. But as grandparents, a higher degree of vicariousness is usually called for, if they are to enjoy the development of young people at a distance. And as grandparents, they also have to diffuse their empathic participation in the development of others over a much wider number. This necessity for taking a parental attitude toward younger generations can also be viewed as an opportunity. As stated at the beginning, the generalization by citizens of the parental attitude of concern to treating the nation as a single household is a boon to public welfare when it occurs.

The recent growth of delight in family life, while it may among parents seem to preoccupy them with private affairs, can among the grandparents who are so much increasing in numbers result in a wider and deeper concept of citizenship. The White House Conference on Children and Youth, therefore, ought to be of equal interest to all generations, not least to the oldest.

For those whose lives encompass the decades of these conferences, the succession of decades, each with its separate emphasis, thus presents a challenge to vicarious participation in the outlooks of each cohort of their successors; it also calls for an effort of philosophical integration. It has often been noted that grandparents sometimes understand their grandchildren better than they did their own children, so there is no reason to despair that the dramatic transitions from generation to generation, so important in the definition of limits and aspirations, are impossible to assimilate. Each in his own full time has a different set of generational perspectives to reconcile with those he embodied in his own young adult commitments. Thus no one is denied, each has his own responsibility to declare where the whole procession is and ought to be headed. Depression and war make us conscious that we are each dependent on all the others but they cannot take from us that we are the integrators who weave from the many strands of influence and experience the particular adult we have become. The old generation has provided the new with the materials of which it must fashion its existence; there are no other available to it. The world stage and the national are set with greater possibilities and fewer limits than any previous actors have entered upon, and thereby inevitably greater dangers. It will be a breathtaking decade in which to participate, directly and vicariously.

In 1930, when I graduated from high school, the commencement speaker chose to expound a pagan text, "When the gods rain gold, O Youth, spread wide thy mantle." His prophecy, then premature, may now be timely.

RURAL YOUTH

by JOHN H. KOLB

FAMILY and community are the nearly universal framework within which youth view themselves and look to their futures. Rural families and their farms continue to serve as seed-beds producing surplus food, fiber, and children. The North American farm family has high value ratings in the tradition of the nation. Rural communities are the exchange and experience arenas for those youth who remain in them and for those who go out to seek their fortune elsewhere.

Both rural life and agriculture now provide their own "challenge of change," contributing to and receiving from others. They never were as isolated and as static as romantic writers have described them. The "revolution," as some characterize current changes, dates to World War II when "Food Will Win the War" and "Food for Freedom" were more than slogans. They represented a social movement, an aroused determination, an impetus to set up scientific research, to apply modern technologies to farming, and to expand production plants. They were the signals for agriculture

John H. Kolb is Professor Emeritus of Rural Sociology at the University of Wisconsin.

to assume and to ask for a place of recognition and respect in the eyes of the nation and of the world. The stereotype of the farmer as the man with a hoe disappeared.

In that period two new concepts, now matured and accepted, were born: agricultural parity and social security. Farmers demanded a "fair share" of the nation's income, and during the ensuing decade the means of achieving this parity have plagued politicians, ensnared congressmen, riven farm leaders and farmer organizations into factions, and have bewildered rural youth beyond possible assessment.

Periods of rapid change in a society can be particularly perplexing to youth when they themselves are undergoing changes—changes of maturity, outlook on the world, decision-making, family relations, and community influences. Young people need time and a degree of stability around them in order to become a part of adult life and to build their own personalities. Denied these they may be thrown into uncertainties or set adrift by indecision. The swirl of changes within the family framework which now involves rural youth can be described briefly in two movements: population mobility and the change from agriculture to agribusiness.

Migration Movements

North American rural society has always been highly mobile. Before the 1930s the movements from the rural seed-beds included the vast trek of people who populated the cities. During the economic disaster of the 1930s, there was a reversal of the urbanward trend which sent many families and many young people back to the land—land that by any standard may have been marginal in production capacity. Since 1940 the movement toward urban centers has resumed but this time only toward, not into, the cities themselves. There at the urban peripheries rural migrants seeking another farm or some other occupational opportunity have been met by families moving from the city centers—a two-way movement converging to form new family patterns and new community arrangements. By 1958 government reports indicated that the rural nonfarm residents, those living in the open-country or places of less than 2,500 population but not on farms, represented one-quarter of the nation's people, while less than 12 percent lived on farms. This means that, in many areas and even in whole states, the rural nonfarm population exceeds the farm.

To complicate the problem of definition and to blur still more distinctions between rural and urban, farmers are increasingly engaged in nonfarm work. By 1957 it was reported that only 35 percent of the nation's farmers were wholly dependent upon agriculture. In that year nearly 3 million farm residents were working off their farms, mainly at nonfarm work, and slightly more than a third of them were farm women working away from their homes. Because 40 percent of the farmers account for about 90 percent of the nation's agricultural production, it follows that the majority of farmers are not confined to their farms occupationally or socially. But, they never were. In earlier years farmers worked on the roads to pay off some of their taxes, bartered in villages and towns for their supplies, and exchanged work with neighbors at planting, threshing, or barn-raising times.

For rural youth migration movements were and are severely selective processes, and this gives them their real significance. Rural to urban migration begins at about age sixteen and is largely over by age thirty. Rates vary with urban conditions and distances. Girls leave rural areas, especially farms, in disproportionally larger numbers than do boys, and at an earlier age. Boys, while less migratory than girls, travel greater distances, and the greater the distance a youth moves the more likely he is to go to some larger city. At least 50 percent of farm youth move to other occupations and to other communities. It is claimed that the expense of rearing and educating country boys and girls who live and work in cities during their productive years is an undue burden. Such claims may be more difficult to maintain in recent years with increased school aid programs, reallocation of some income and special taxes to localities, and the rising costs of farm subsidies and surplus storages.

Family-wise the selective migration takes more younger families than older ones and more of those who were operators of small rather than large farms. Tenant farm families lose more of their youth to cities than do owner families. Also, families with a number of community organization connections are less mobile than those with few such contacts. From every angle family and community are interrelated in their influences upon youth.

Qualitative aspects of these migration movements are probably even more important for society than the quantitative. In this regard there is less agreement in opinion and in research results than about the extent of the movements.

One interpretation is that the deviants leave the country for the city—the more and the less capable. Another is that farm youth are the "left-behinds," either by indecision, inertia, or low aspiration. There is evidence of relatively low levels of urban labor-market achievement by farm-reared youth, and that those rural youth who do migrate tend to have completed more years of schooling and have higher intelligence test scores than do those who remain in rural areas. These variations in estimates change with time and place, with definitions of capabilities, and with values attributed to results of various testing techniques. Some of the implications for decision-making by rural youth will be considered later.

The issue in this connection for policy-making and for continued study is how to help rural youth reorient toward the larger society of which they are to be part and parcel—not a drab, leveled-out, mass industrial society, but one of opportunities at various levels of interest, achievement, ability, and relative advantages. The traditional rubric of a rural-urban dichotomy is no longer relevant for youth either of country or of city birth. The city must have the products of the various seed-beds to supply itself with food, fiber, and workers of many kinds; and the country needs the feedback from the city of machinery, insecticides, artificial fertilizers, merchandise, and skilled workers and specialists. But to pit one segment of society against another because of differences in residence, occupation, or cultural values is inferior statesmanship. Rural youth are in need, just now, of a reinterpretation regarding the interrelationships in society. This will take a bit of doing since attitudes of opposition and contrast are deep-seated. Country parents express fears and offer resistances to having their children go away to the city for work or for school and these attitudes can often be detected in the reactions of rural youth to new situations. The old myth that the country is God-given and the city devil-derived is not easily dispelled.

Rethinking is also required at professional and theoretical levels. Newer theoretical constructs than the traditional "rural" and "urban" are needed, for neither includes all of a kind, surely not as of now, if indeed they ever did. Only when other variables are introduced can real meanings in an analysis be gained—variations in education levels, in parental experiences, in occupational opportunities, in incomes, in geographic regions, in social status. Moreover, such variables occur in complexes, combinations, syndromes. Analyses by simple dichotomies are too often misleading since there may be greater differences within each category than between them.

Agribusiness

A second movement immediately involving rural youth is from agriculture to agribusiness. In academic circles agribusiness is defined as including not only production on farms and ranches but the processing and distributing of the commodities so produced, and also the manufacturing and distributing of supplies and equipment used in the production. These services have expanded to unrealized proportions and provide occupational opportunities for millions of rural farm, nonfarm, and city people.

There is a striking similarity between the up-curves of those engaged in agribusiness and the down-curves of those in agriculture in its traditional sense. Between 1929 and 1953 all workers on farms in the United States decreased by more than 3 million while workers in the marketing of farm products increased nearly 2 million. Agribusiness is reported to account for 40 percent of all consumer expenditures and to employ 37 percent of the labor force.

At the farming end of the process rapid changes have been in full swing for some time. Within commercial agriculture improved technologies and results of research have resulted in great increases in outputs per acre, per animal, per farm, and per farmer. Reports from government sources show that the physical volume of farm products in 1956 was about 50 percent above that of twenty-five years earlier. The size of farms increased 40 percent in fifteen years to 336 acres in 1954, while farm population decreased about 28 percent from 1940 to 1954. But changes occurred not only on farms but among farmers through numerous contractual arrangements. One of these features is termed "vertical integration." A farmer who operates within such an arrangement shares with one or more related businesses some of his management decisions and risks in both the producing and the marketing of his commodities.

Commercial farmers are also involved in other contractual arrangements through sales and bargaining associations, cooperative organizations for production, marketing and purchasing, through governmental inspections for sanitation and maintaining standards, and through agreements under

parity provisions. Thus with the benefits of improved technologies, contract and integration plans, and with government policies for parity, present-day agriculture has piled up
previously unheard of surpluses. Agriculture now finds itself
operating in an economy of abundance with a theory of
scarcity.

Some results of such rapid and often chaotic changes are
brought into focus by a statement made by a group of
younger-than-average agricultural economists.[1] They had been
meeting for discussions under the auspices of the Social Science Research Council and were thus free to state the case
as they regarded it professionally, not as the representatives
of their respective employing institutions or agencies. They
considered the period of change as critical and "the response
of agriculture as confused." The statement emphasized that
there is a welcoming and rapid adoption of some changes
and a resistance to others that may be inevitable concomi-
tants. A recognition that moral as well as economic values
are involved in the troubled situation is very heartening.

Some consequences of the changes pointed out in the statement include: chronic distress in certain sections of agriculture in spite of public remedial measures that have grown
to unmanageable size and accelerated movements of people
out of agriculture; a widening of the income gap among
those families who remain, between those able to adopt new

[1] George K. Brinegar, Kenneth L. Bachman, and Herman M. South-
worth, "Reorientations in Research in Agricultural Economics," Report
of the Subcommittee of the Social Science Research Council Committee
on Agricultural Economics, *Journal of Farm Economics*, Vol. XLI, No. 3
(August 1959), pp. 600–19.

technologies and those lacking financial resources or personal capabilities; and successive areas of agriculture being increasingly controlled by outside commercial interests.

"Problem-Farming"

Chronic distress areas and those farming families which cannot close the income gap are likewise a part of the agricultural picture which rural youth must view and seek to understand when decisions are being made. These areas and families represent nearly one-half of the farm population of the nation; 48 percent was the estimate reported to Congress in 1955 by the United States Department of Agriculture. This "other half" of agriculture does not come within the compass of the rapidly changing conditions just described for commercial agriculture. Its families live in "low-income," "subsistence," or "problem-farming" areas. The various terms have similar meanings. More than four-fifths of the farms in "low-income" areas had gross sales of less than $2,500 in 1949. The concept, "low-income" farmer, is relatively new but however defined, it includes a heterogeneous group of people and represents multiple problems. The most significant fact about low-income families is that they are concentrated and they have remained remarkably stable over the years.

"Problem areas" include a majority of the rural population referred to as "minority groups": Negroes, Spanish-speaking peoples, and Indians. Many are tenants, share-croppers, and those on small farms. These are the source for regular or seasonal labor for owners and operators of larger farms.

"Problem" farm families contribute heavily to the manpower of the nation. Between 1940 and 1954 an estimated one-half of the expansion in the nonagricultural labor force was supplied by movements from the farm population and more than half of this came from low-income farming areas. The proportion of children and youth under twenty years of age is much higher in these areas, and the proportion in the productive adult ages is lower than in the rest of the farm population. Some of the families are welfare cases because of sickness, age, or broken homes.

Problems are multiple because of limited physical resources, small farming units, inadequate health protection, and children handicapped in educational opportunities. Institutional, cultural, and family patterns of attitudes and values seem to hem in these families, setting them apart. To rescue them from their own sense of low status and to improve actual opportunities for youth especially, is a major issue. Improvement programs are now under way and are meeting with success, according to government reports, but methods used for communicating with commercial farm families are not effective with the problem families. Mass media do not "reach" them. They are not members of the usual farmer organizations and their educational achievement levels limit their use of circulars and bulletins. They require more personal approaches through informal groups, including friends and neighbors.

The "boot-strap" methods, aimed at helping families to help themselves, appear to have limitations unless changes in some of the fundamental sources of the difficulties can be brought about. The question can be raised as to how long agriculture can endure half commercial, half problem.

Migrant, seasonal, transient laborer families moving in and out of the problem and other areas, serving as an accepted or considered a necessary adjunct to commercial farming in certain regions, defy description. To report that their children and youth are slow and irregular in school progress, do not participate in social activities, are not accepted by others, are often handicapped by poor health and by emotional disturbances, and that parents display seemingly little interest, is only to understate the case.

On the more hopeful and encouraging side, it can be stated that improvements are under way—more and better health clinics, medical care, camp accommodations and sanitation, provisions for food, transportation of children to specially built schools, services by churches and grants from private foundations for studies. A real promise in the situation is the surprising response on the part of children when favorable opportunities are provided. Also, by more mechanization and diversification on larger farms and ranches and within communities, the worker families are becoming somewhat less migrant. They tend to form into colonies and to settle in substandard houses on the outskirts of towns and cities. These settlements become like Toonerville, California, which gradually, over the years, evolve into a Farmersville with their own respectable schools, churches, stores, taverns, and social organizations. But there are heavy social and economic costs and sacrifices of human resources along the way. On the other hand, some of the "foreigner" laborer families of yesterday who were denied the privilege of swimming in the community pool have sons who today are wealthy farm owners and members of school and church boards. Many do not.

Career Plans

Rural youth are caught in these changing complexes of confusion and contradiction: agriculture to agribusiness, family farming to vertical integration, traditional attitudes of individualism to power politics with attempted production regulations and ridiculous surpluses, widening gaps between commercial and problem farming, and inland isolation to world military strategy. In the midst of all this and their elders' indecision, they must, sooner or later, answer the question: to farm or not to farm?

Decision-making has engaged the time, energy, and finances, not only of many rural youth, but of many researchers, especially since 1950. Before that time studies concerned with rural youth usually centered about selective migration, attitudes in regard to farming, and their apparent reactions to local problems. The more recent studies indicate that farm-reared youth who migrate to cities are relatively unsuccessful or reach only low levels of achievement in many urban occupations. This has real significance since it is estimated that about one-third of nonfarm people in the whole country were reared on farms. Low levels of aspiration in regard to occupation and education are also known to be related with low levels of achievement. Therefore, the rather widely accepted conclusion of some researchers that nonfarm youth have higher educational aspirations than do farm youth of equal intelligence has important implications.

Other studies suggest, however, that perhaps most of the difference between aspiration levels of farm and nonfarm youth can be accounted for by the low aspirations of farm boys who plan to farm. Much depends upon the meaning given to the concept "aspiration." If it means to desire something which one does not possess, then the farm boy who plans to farm is not in the race to get somewhere else. His planning to farm may have been by deliberate decision or by default of indecision. In either case the results may be tragic. If he should change his mind because of new experiences or of recognized inability to keep or to gain a foothold in farming, he is unprepared for other possible opportunities. He is likely to move into lower levels of occupation than his abilities could permit, because he lacks the necessary education and training for the higher levels. The loss is not only his, personally, but society fails to realize a potential resource.

This kind of situation is not difficult to visualize or to experience. Financial resources may not be available when $30,000 to $50,000 is needed to acquire ownership of some middle-range farms. Or some farm-reared youth may fall victim to what is termed "effective environment." They become accustomed to and oriented toward the lifeways and the social values which agriculture represents to them. Their casual contacts with other ways of life and work may even have blunted their desire to change. They are bombarded with the same kinds of movies, comics, TV programs, and other mass media but it doesn't "take." Studies indicate that many perceptions are limited within various group relations: peer groups, those of about the same age and social status; reference groups, those whose approval is sought and whose values are accepted; primary groups, those whose responses are personal, intimate, and considered important for personality development.

The planning-not-to-farm side of the story is fully as important as the planning-to-farm, especially as the trends in migration continue. This, the researchers point out, is more than a negation but must be considered as part of "an act" to enter the nonfarming world. Three factors are suggested which may result in this kind of planning: certain personality characteristics probably associated with early training, perceiving farming as unattainable for them, and being sons of parents who are more oriented to the nonfarm than to the farm world.

From every source of evidence parents and families are implicated in youth decisions: parents of those youth who plan not to farm have higher levels of education and occupation aspirations for their sons than do parents of those who plan to farm; socio-economic levels of families have an influence on children's desire for education; family background is a factor bearing on chances for academic survival; parents' participation is associated with the "drop-outs" in 4H Club youth groups; years of schooling completed by parents are associated with attitudes toward the education of their children. These and other conclusions even suggest the necessity of an early and deliberate breakup of sons' expectations that they can or should be farmers.

Many decisions may not be direct and in a straight line. Everyone familiar with rural youth recognizes that questions are often settled piece by piece, that the process may be complex and often takes a long time. Once set in train, decisions do move on but compromises and reasons are often mixed with what may appear to be fortuitous circumstances.

Open Questions

Issues involved in the context of this section of the discussion are many and complicated. Only a few will be reviewed and perhaps in too brief and idealistic phrases to suggest solutions, practical or workable. They will follow in reverse order to that of the discussion.

First, "more research is needed." This expression is found in nearly every report examined. Results reported need to be retested under different conditions and with other groups of people. Simple and direct answers to problems of decision-making are being demanded from many sources but the issue is how to be more certain of results for special application, and how to communicate those which are dependable to points of real need. Many questionnaires are being circulated among rural youth but replies of "father," "mother," "friend," "teacher," to questions regarding early influences on decisions may, upon more intensive investigation, turn out to be rationalizations, escapes from pressures to think, or be substitutes for actual unknowns.

More attention might well be turned to the area of discovery. How can rural youth be exposed through experiences to other than the farm environment? How to "stir up the gift that is within thee"? Are determinations once aroused and abilities discovered transferable to other areas of action previously considered latent, retarded, or even nonexistent? Studies are needed not only for their predictive purposes but for the more rapid improvement of facilities and personnel for counseling and for guidance at early ages.

What can be done to compensate for the low levels of education attainment on the part of farm parents? Reports indicate that nearly one-third of the nation's farmers had only an eighth-grade or less schooling. Now a high-school education is the expected level in rural society; but as was pointed out, studies show high correlation between schooling of parents and their attitudes and ambitions toward the education of their children.

Second is the issue of the fuller development of rural youth as society's great human resource. Agriculture might well give greater attention to this problem of human resources in whatever seed-beds they may have grown. A Congressional committee was told recently that the "hard core" of the farm problem is the surplus of human effort committed to farming. "Interdependence," within a national as well as an international economy, would appear to be a signpost which should be followed. How can agriculture continue trying to be separate and self-concerned, while attempting to rid itself of its own surpluses, human and material? Can such surpluses be somehow regarded as an opportunity instead of a problem? "Free-the-World-from-Hunger," is a movement proposed by the Food and Agriculture Organization of the United Nations, whose recently appointed director-general is a citizen of India, and should know whereof he speaks.

Third is the issue of how to shift some emphasis from economic production to social and personal development. There is much agreement that technologies alone will not solve all problems, but just how to shift into other channels is not at all clear or agreed upon. The truth that man cannot live by bread alone requires reemphasis with each new turn of human affairs. How can cultural values long associated with farm family living be kept unless they are given away, shared with other families—families with which farm youth will inevitably be associating—merchant families, professional families, worker families, industrial families?

Families and communities in rural society are indissoluble. Communities are families in their interdependent relationships—the framework for their youth in action. Migration movements and business farming have their counterparts in changing community relations. Two trends, among others, will be singled out for review here: the increasing interdependences of communities and the growing institutional pressures.

During the earlier periods of rural society, country neighborhoods, often relatively isolated from general society, exerted strong influences upon youth to conform to local group values and patterns of behavior. Many open-country neighborhoods have succumbed to succeeding social movements but a surprising number of the hamlet neighborhoods have survived. Some are stronger and more active than they were ten or fifteen years ago. They are more economic in their orientation than in former years and they are also more varied in the character of their influences.

For older rural youth, hamlets provide much more contact points with the outside world than earlier since not only friends but passers-by meet there. Their influences upon children must not be overlooked, especially in the so-called "problem areas" and in the small settlements on the outskirts of towns and cities. Even in the areas of commercial agriculture they serve as channels for communication and for evaluating changes. They are capable of two-way action: implementing innovations of certain kinds and protecting members from too abrupt changes when accepted modes of behavior or established beliefs seem challenged. Recent studies indicate that they have most meaning for those youth and adults who actually participate in their activities since then identification becomes action.

Village-country or town-country communities have emerged as centers of influence in rural society. However, the movement is not completed even though as population aggregates they appear to be well established. Many farmers and ranchers live in the village or town centers and some business and professional families are country residents, yet many differing interests are not fully reconciled. There are external evidences of an integrated group, but upon examination there are indications of lack of the internal requirements for community solidarity and for unified action. There are overlapping administrations and areas for elementary and secondary schools, for health and hospital services, fire and police protection, sewage disposal and water supply. In some cases, efforts for community coordination have been so strong that an ambition for self-sufficiency has developed. This tendency has made it difficult for one community to work with another for their larger mutual interests.

Of increasing importance are the nonfarm families which come to take up residence. The newcomers are less responsive than earlier residents to the personal relations with local merchants and organization officers. They go readily to other larger centers for shopping and for recreation, even religious services.

Recent population movements toward but not into cities tend to converge about centers as small as 5,000. Many smaller places, especially of less than 1,000 population, are experiencing difficulties in their social and economic adjustments to changing times.

Thus, current movements of centralization and decentralization of population, agriculture, and industry tend to meet at the crossroads of larger town-country communities and at the peripheries of cities. This defines the most important current trend in rural community relations—the increasing interdependence of communities. The desires and struggles for local community self-sufficiency and independence have been and still are very strong, especially where the processes of town and country coordination have not been fully achieved. However, many readjustments are under way among communities of varying sizes and character and these have special significance for rural youth. First of all, it is quite evident that certain social and economic services and institutions belong together within the same communities.

The trend is moving toward a clustering of certain kinds of services and a differentiating of various communities into recognized types. Plans for community development must take into account the fact that some types of communities can establish or maintain certain kinds of services and institutions, but for others they must look to other communities and assume their share of responsibility and support. Some rural communities are finding this principle of interdependence difficult to follow. As pointed out before, they seem to feel a sense of moral responsibility to provide all things for all their people, even to furnishing employment for all their maturing youth. This simply cannot be done. To attempt to supply inferior or inadequate facilities for education, recreation, religion, or other needed services in order to be "loyal to the home town" is to short-change youth.

Responses of rural youth to these changing community relations are encouraging and often refreshing. They are doing things and going places which the adults may be doing later. Those youth in smaller communities are going to larger centers for such contacts as recreation, without apologies although not always with full parental consent. Correlations were found between size of resident community and declared intention of occupational choices and with desired future residences.

Casual conversations with young people, especially of high-school ages, often bring forth complaints regarding lack of work opportunities, restricted recreational opportunities, and impatience with conservative adult attitudes. More extended discussions usually reveal recognitions of many community conditions and limitations and a real concern for the future of the communities and their own plans for further education and full employment. Checking daily schedules often showed many activities even during summer vacation periods and a multiplicity of school and church-related organization contacts during the academic year. Complaints were encountered among some families that these activities encroached upon family life. Uneven responses were found among youth to the various special interest groups and organizations represented locally. Many of the same variables were associated with the differences among adults. The mothers' reactions were often most predictive of family patterns.

A second important trend in rural community relations is the growing dominance and central orientation of formally organized groups and institutions. Since 1950 many rural organizations, both public and private, have secured the services of professional and paid personnel on a county-wide basis and with state and national affiliations. These trends often result in degrees of uniformity in organization procedures and the creation of power structures capable of controlling channels of communication and of exerting outside pressures upon the local groups concerned. Similar tendencies are even more discernible among many local community institutions such as schools, churches, businesses, and centrally organized farmer associations.

The tendency to be self-centered and self-sufficient was observed among churches during recent restudies of country neighborhoods and town-country communities. There were evidences of overlapping church areas, of church contacts criss-crossing community boundaries and of country churches operating without regard to those in nearby villages or towns. Families were traveling greater distances than in former years, seeking churches of their preference. Many differing sects were being formed, often among former, dissident members of locally established churches. These and other evidences would suggest that organized religious interests are being directed toward churches as institutions rather than toward communities as social groups. If this interpretation is warranted, many questions arise.

Some church leaders are making ardent pleas that churches must perform their community functions in order to survive. Others contend that the church should recreate the community in its own image; while others, concerned with transcendental relations, would keep aloof from the world.

A recent study showed that the "effective" churches were markedly superior to the average churches in respect to their community outlooks, that village churches rated higher in this respect than country churches, and that town churches rated higher than village churches. Among the "effective" churches the index of community relations diminished as the members of the suborganizations of the churches increased.

Tendencies similar in effect were found among some educational institutions in town-country communities. Much attention is given to policies proposed by outside central agencies. Some high schools in agribusiness communities have continued programs, both agricultural and academic, designed for past needs rather than for today's demands on rural youth. Offerings are too limited in scope and content to prepare them for expanded opportunities. In many such cases the village boy is the forgotten one since he can not usually qualify for the vocational courses because he does not have home projects available. If he does not plan to go on to college, many of the academic subjects do not appeal to him.

Branch banks and branch mercantile establishments in town-country communities have many policies and prices fixed at central headquarters. Their managers live and work in the communities but are often, not always, less identified with the local affairs than are the owner-operators of similar businesses. Industries which are much sought after by rural communities in order to provide local work opportunities usually hire employees without regard to their residences. Their managers say that they are compelled to do this because certain skills are needed and it is simpler to try to find them wherever they are than to set up local training programs. Such policies often leave only the unskilled jobs for local people. They may likewise have little regard for local customs and traditions, when, for example, they run the plant Saturdays and Sundays during the fruit and vegetable harvest.

Some of the larger and stronger farmer organizations are no longer the social, economic, or even the local marketing agencies they once were. They have become more largely pressure groups for the protection of special agricultural interests and have their paid lobbyists and their favored legislative programs at state and national levels.

If it be true that local institutions and organizations are

becoming more oriented toward themselves and their special interests, rather than to the communities of which they are a part, then it may be proposed as a basis for study that rural youth are faced with a number of alternative choices: 1) They may compartmentalize, make little or no effort at reconciliation of various teachings and value positions of the different institutions in the community. They may open and shut mental and emotional doors as they go from one to the other. 2) They may recognize and verbalize the conflicts which they experience, or the inconsistencies may lie below the surface, unrealized and unexpressed but disturbing. 3) They may invent procedures of their own and go merrily on their ways with ideas and actions which are quite deviant from those publicly accepted by adults in the community. 4) They may not be influenced or stimulated because the local institutions and organizations are silent on important community issues.

Illustrations of all these alternatives were observed during recent restudies of town-country communities. Conflicts between schools and churches were most easily recognized. In one community high-school girls were presenting petitions signed not only by parents but by church pastors, in order to be excused from certain physical education activities and regulations. In another community a small church building with a large neon-lighted cross stood across the street from the school. The principal of the school said he paid no attention to the church and that it did not influence his pupils. Conversations with the pupils put his conclusions in doubt. One community had within its area a country church whose members observed Saturday rather than Sunday as their Sabbath. Conflicts arose over when ball games and concerts should be scheduled. Another community had a large and dominant church with many organizations and activities for its young people. Non-church youth in the community complained that these interfered with and restricted school-related social programs.

The discussion in this section can be summed up by suggesting that relations of rural youth with their communities may take at least three forms: personal—the extent to which they feel accepted in the community; social—the extent to which their acceptance is converted into participation; moral—the extent to which their behavior is responsive to community norm-values.

Issues for policy-making and for further studying are also many and varied. Only two are offered here, and in brief and general terms. First, creativity in youth is the call of the day. Industry, especially, is asking for creative ability in its scientists and its engineers, and is devising batteries of tests to find it as if it were a hidden treasure needing only discovery to be exploited. How are special abilities once discovered to find expression? Youth are encouraged to be different, to assert themselves, to question education's teachings and religious beliefs. The issue presents itself as to whether schools and other established institutions can, under pressure of crowded conditions, provide opportunities and experiences which are as agreeable to the dissenter as to the conformist.

Second, and corollary to the first, youth, it is important to recall, are involuntary members of families and communities, at least in the beginning of their lives. As suggested earlier in regard to farm boys, youth do not have the freedom for choices which some research designs seem to assume. Their recognized alternatives are limited, but as they mature their desire for independence comes to the fore. There are those who believe that this independence can be best achieved within an atmosphere of confidence—confidence in the general aims and objectives of one's society. Some educators are saying that they should be more sure and articulate regarding their own aims and the roles their schools should play in contemporary communities. Without these their pupils and parents lose confidence in them.

Some political scientists are urging the need for more overall positive belief in the American system rather than for isolated refutations of the details of other ideologies. The issue, then, for rural youth in their community relations is how to secure proper balance between the need for self-confident independence and the need for social control.

NEGRO YOUTH IN THE SOUTH

by LEWIS W. JONES

CHILDREN in the South today, both white and Negro, are in circumstances such as few other generations of children have known. In some periods of change or crisis children have been cast in bewildering roles as victims of action to which they were in no way a party. Southern children today are in social situations where they must make precocious decisions about their own conduct. Influencing these decisions are interaction between children, interaction between children and adults who have different relationships to them, and an awareness of judgments being passed on them by those who observe their conduct from nearby and from afar. There is an urgency upon children of the South to choose between alternative expectations of them. The responsibility placed upon these children makes the past ten years fateful ones for the future of the South in ways that many people may not comprehend because of their intense involvement with a particular point of view or preoccupation with a selected sequence of events.

Lewis W. Jones is Director of Social Science Research, College of Arts and Sciences, Tuskegee Institute.

Children and youth have known the impact of an ideological controversy in which there have been massive efforts at persuasion to one or another point of view about the values of this society. Southern children have had to give heed to passionate indoctrination directed specifically at them. Their introduction to our social institutions, especially our political institutions, has been quite different from that given other generations of children. The general and somewhat idealized textbook descriptions may be essentially the same as before but through the mass media and from interpretations by their elders these institutions are made to appear quite different and often far from ideal. The conclusions they reach about the society and government will influence the kind of citizens they become.

Negro children all over the South are now making a fateful commitment about themselves as persons, as are all young Southerners who have had to face up to questions regarding who they are and what their futures may be. During the past decade the status of the Negro child in the South became an issue characterized by unprecedented controversy in the course of which Negro children and youth came to new conceptions of their roles in American society. Changes in the status of the Negro child are functionally related to basic culture changes in the nation and in the Southern region, including technological and economic changes, changes in social structure and organization, and changes in the value system and belief patterns. In four major areas improvement of the status of the Negro child has come to be a critical issue for the society.

1. *Manpower*. Post-war evaluations of the availability and

use of the nation's manpower resources during mobilization
for World War II, both for military service and for manning
the productive machinery, brought the knowledge and skills
of Negroes under intense scrutiny.

2. *Citizenship.* Hardly less significant is the citizenship
status of Negroes in the ideological contest between the
United States and Russia for support in Asia and Africa. The
United States need not disavow the disadvantages past and
present generations of Negroes have known if it can demonstrate improved opportunities offered oncoming generations.

3. *Education.* Preoccupation with the quality of education
given American youth inescapably emphasized the lag of the
education of Negro youth behind national and regional
norms.

4. *Productive Potential.* Technological and social changes
in the South brought a migration of population from the
region to other areas of the country where the productive
inadequacies and social disabilities of migrants produced
critical community problems. The experiences of migrants
in their formative years in the South are held accountable for
the problems they present wherever they go.

For Negro youth to share in programs to remove inequali-
ties between the Southern region and the rest of the nation,
essential conditions for Negro participation had to be established. In the process of redefinition of the status of the Negro
child no component of the American institutional structure
has been exempt although the courts assumed the major responsibility in prescribing a basic legal status contrary to
legal precedent and entrenched custom.

An acute self-consciousness might be expected on the part

pectancy. Their lives were lived out in a state of dependence in which major decisions as to their fortunes and those of their children were not theirs to make. If poverty and illiteracy were not effective controls, economic pressure, punitive legal action, and threat of extra-legal punishment were. There were gradations of economic positions above this lowest level that carried prestige on the Negro side of the color line. These higher status positions within the Southern social system, however, carried with them an obligation to be useful to whites, bear symbols of inferiority, and obey the etiquette prescribed for subordinate-superordinate relationships. Cowed lower-status Negroes and cynical upper-status Negroes so conducted themselves as to allow whites to enjoy an illusion of "good race relations."

As the group above the lower stratum grew in numbers Negro children were taught how to advance to these better positions. The Negro child had to acquire the social skills essential to effective functioning in this society if he expected to live in it. The upwardly aspiring Negro child had to acquire a finely balanced equilibrium, maintain security and preferential treatment from the white South, press always for a better overall Negro status, and keep the opportunities of the broad American culture in focus as aspiration targets.

This was the situation in the late '30s, when Charles S. Johnson presented his observations of youth in the South in *Growing Up in the Black Belt*. Challenges to the Southern social order were then neither boldly open nor aggressive. There was considerable social ferment within the Negro culture that was having its influence on the personality development of Negro youth. Some of his observations were:

No group in America, however, is experiencing a more rapid or profound internal change in its social composition than the Negro group. Over a comparatively brief period the cultural level of this group has been considerably advanced. Illiteracy and mortality rates have declined markedly, the standard of living has been raised to some extent, there has been a pronounced advance in the organization of family life, and there have been other equally significant changes. The external evidences of improvement have been accompanied by a less conspicuous but nevertheless intense struggle of the members of the group for position and recognition within the group. Negro youth are a part of this bitter struggle, and the period of adolescence is one in which the tensions engendered by feelings of personal inadequacy and social insecurity register their most violent shocks. . . .

The race system in the South is preserved by legal sanctions and the threat of physical violence, quite as much as by the mutual acceptance of traditional modes of behavior. Furthermore, the attitudes of the white group are constantly changing and at many points in the relationship between the two races there is a blurring of caste distinctions. In general the Negro continues to occupy a subordinate position, but the fact that he is struggling against this status rather than accepting it, and that the white group is constantly redefining its own status in relation to the Negro, indicates that in the future if one cannot safely predict progress in race relations, he can at least predict change.[2]

Change

The hopes of Negro youth today about their tomorrow are in striking contrast to the hopes their fathers held. Negroes below the age of twenty in 1960 know what immediate drastic change means. These children see respected Negro adults

[2] Charles S. Johnson, *Growing Up in the Black Belt* (Washington, D.C.: American Council on Education, American Youth Commission Studies, 1940).

and courageous Negro children in front page news, in contrast to the customary practice of ignoring Negroes except
for criminal acts. The quickened concern of Southern legis-
latures over their education, heretofore long neglected, has
projected Negro children into a sudden prominence they
had never known. They realize the eyes of the world are on
this drama as it unfolds with Negro children playing stellar
roles for the first time in their lives, supported or opposed,
as the case may be, by their white contemporaries as they
make their personal decisions in a new relationship. This
generation of children lives in a climate of change and they
will increasingly influence its course.

The greatest change since 1940 has been the redefinition
of the Negro's legal status in the South through a succession
of judicial decisions that progressed from removal of specific
negative legal sanctions to a positive affirmation of legal
protection of common opportunity for Americans without
distinction.

Changes in the status of Negroes in the South have come
about as they could only come—with sweeping internal
changes in the South as the economic and political positions
of the South underwent change. The cultural gap between
Negro Southerners and white Southerners has narrowed as
has the gap between all Southerners and the rest of the nation. The New Deal, World War II, post-war economic
prosperity, and the role of the United States in international
affairs have all had their impact on the South in bringing
greater cultural consistency in the region and that of the
region in the nation. The changing citizenship status of

Negroes in the South has been influenced by their economic
advances and both citizenship and economic statuses have
been influenced by the Negro's changing educational status.

The economic status of Southern Negroes has greatly improved despite the fact that it has not improved as much as
the economic status of whites who have favored employment
opportunity. Urban Negro families earning less than $1,000
annually decreased from 90 to 40 percent from 1936 to
1949. By 1954, the median annual income of urban Negroes
in the South was $2,425, which was 56 percent of the median
income of urban whites. The median incomes of both rural
farm whites and rural farm Negroes remained low in 1954,
with the $749 median for Negroes being 49 percent of the
median for whites. However, the fact that one-half the urban
Negro families in the South had an income of more than
$2,500 indicates a greatly improved economic status over
that suffered by a predominantly rural Negro population
two decades earlier. Increasing recognition of the importance
of the Negro market to the economic well-being of the
region causes Negroes themselves to have consciousness of
the economic power it gives them.

Within the South urbanization has greatly accelerated
since 1940. The increase in the urban Negro population
from 1940 to 1950 (26 percent) was less than that of the
white population (43 percent) since the greater movement
of Negroes was to outside the region. Migration within the
South showed a higher proportion of Negroes who moved
into metropolitan areas going into the central cities than of
whites. The rural areas and the small market towns of the

South continue to be strongholds of that Southern tradition which is least yielding to change in the Negro's status. However, population reduction in such areas is making them less important economically and politically.

The movement of the Negro population and the relative numerical importance of Negroes in different areas in the South are related directly to changes in the opportunities for employment created by changes in the economy of the South.

Students of the Southern scene have documented, statistically, the changes in the South over the past two decades. Their conclusions are in agreement with those of John M. Maclachlan and Joe S. Floyd, Jr., in their volume, *This Changing South* which describes: "strain toward consistency with national levels of economic performance" accompanied by cultural changes as aspects of the same fundamental trend.[3] Trends in the status of Negro Southerners indicate the same strain with especially aggressive action to remove invidious distinctions in their citizenship status. The result is a vitally dynamic conception of their citizenship role on the part of Negroes. Professor William G. Carleton, in the summer 1958 issue of the *Antioch Review*, expressed the view that these changes have improved the Negro status: "Groups once underprivileged and exploited are no longer underprivileged and can no longer be exploited as they were. With rising living standards and educational advantages members of once-exploited groups have come to have more

[3] John M. Maclachlan and Joe S. Floyd, Jr., *This Changing South* (Gainesville: University of Florida Press, 1956).

respect for themselves and they are demanding and getting
more and more respect from others."

Circumstances of cultural change over the past quarter of
a century have produced new functions, new roles, for both
whites and Negroes and new relationship patterns between
them are emerging. The many changes that might be described are affecting the young even more than their elders.
They are learning and experiencing without the need for
unlearning or forgetting. Their normal expectations in many
things exceed the vague fond hopes of their parents' childhood.

Locating the Future

It has become so obvious as to be redundant to say that the
future of very few Negro children is in the rural South. First
of all, children are no longer a productive asset. In most types
of agriculture, particularly in cotton growing, machinery has
made the hand labor of children uneconomical. For many
years schooling was regarded as of little importance for Negro
farm children. Their futures were seen to be in the fields and
the more they worked there the better they could learn what
they needed to know. Farmer parents themselves needed the
labor of their children to add to their poor incomes, and
rationalized keeping them at work rather than in school.
This has changed but there are parents who do not realize
it.

The greatest demand for child workers in the South today
is in vegetable and fruit production which use migratory

workers for brief periods. This problem has been intensively
studied during the past decade and there are agencies actively
working to help children in migratory families who follow
harvests from Florida to North Carolina and on out of the
South to New York State. These are the most disadvantaged
children in the South today. Their experiences threaten
to restrict their futures to the transient life of migratory
workers.

The future of Negro youth in the South, then, is in its
urban areas. By 1950, 74 percent of Southern nonrural Negroes were located in 53 major cities. Maclachlan and Floyd,
projecting past and present population trends, conclude that
by 1970 Southern Negroes will be "predominantly urban and
concentrated heavily in the region's largest metropolitan
areas." Great numbers of Negro children will be urban dwellers outside of the South as a result of recent and current
migration trends.

In 1940 there were 4.5 million Negroes living on farms. In
1950 this number had dropped to 3.4 million and in 1957
the estimated population was 2.8 million.

It has become increasingly difficult to enter farming since
the farm business today requires a considerable sum of capital
as do other business enterprises. Negro youth who aspire to
farming careers will be a highly selected and doubtless a
small group. Those who see their futures as farm laborers will
have to possess skills very different from those their tenant
fathers used. These skills will be mechanical and technical.
As one farmer watching the operation of a cotton harvesting
machine remarked to a visitor, "That boy's got to be smart;

he's settin' on $8,000 of my money." The future of Negro youth in agriculture appears to be in a small class of farm-owner operators and as skilled farm workers.

It has been assumed that by the end of the present decade, if the movement continues, half the total Negro population of this country will be living outside the 13 traditionally Southern states. And half of those remaining in the South will be in urban and predominantly metropolitan areas. Not only will the southern Negroes be in metropolitan areas, but they also will be inside the central cities of those areas. However, a big "if" lately has become attached to this first assumption. Tennessee discovered in the spring of 1957 that whites were moving north as fast as, and perhaps even faster than, Negroes. In March 1957, Dr. Harold A. Pedersen of the Department of Sociology and Rural Life at Mississippi State College reported that between April 1950 and July 1956 Mississippi had lost to migration 80,197 citizens, of whom 51,355 were whites and only 28,842 were Negroes. This sharply reversed a trend that most had believed as recently as 1956 was in the other direction. White urban dwellers in the South as elsewhere have flowed outward to the suburbs. The Negro movement has been to the centers of cities. The 1950 census found that while 63 percent of the white populations of southern metropolitan areas lived inside the central cities, 74 percent of the nonwhites were within the city proper. Six states had almost 80 percent or more of their metropolitan Negro populations inside the central cities rather than in the suburbs, a proportion attained only by Louisiana for the white group.[4]

Since Negro children today may confidently expect futures in urban communities, what kind of future awaits them there? The Negro migrants who have been on the move to

[4] Donald Shoemaker et al., *With All Deliberate Speed* (New York: Harper, 1957), p. 72.

urban centers increasingly since the outbreak of World War II, continue to move there. As these Negro children change residence from rural to urban areas they become beneficiaries of educational opportunities, recreational facilities, and health and welfare services superior to those available in the poorer communities from which they have migrated.

A logical conclusion to follow the prospect of urbanization is that in view of the dramatic increase in industrial plants in the South the Negro child of today may expect industrial employment. However, his opportunities for employment as an industrial worker are not too promising.

Eli Ginzberg in *The Negro Potential* [5] has described the advancement and limitations on advancement of Negroes in nonagricultural employment in the South. Between 1940 and 1950 nonagricultural employment in the South expanded by almost 60 percent for white women, almost 40 percent for white men, 30 percent for Negro men and only 7 percent for Negro women. Negroes have not been employed in the new industries locating in the South in anything like their proportion of the labor force. Ginzberg cites the Southern automobile industry as employing over 10,000 white men as operatives but fewer than 350 Negro men. However, the employment of Negroes even at occupational levels lower than those of whites in cities is a distinct advancement over their previous agricultural employment. On the basis of this employment in cities the Negro middle class has grown with

[5] Eli Ginzberg et al., *The Negro Potential* (New York: Columbia University Press, 1956).

more Negroes in professional, semiprofessional and service occupations which primarily serve the Negro population.

As the number of man-hours necessary to produce consumer goods is progressively reduced, employment in the future must be sought in types of jobs other than in manufacturing industries. Expanding opportunities are appearing in the service occupations. Opportunities in this field for Negro youth are small because traditionally there have been no apprenticeships for young Negroes in business establishments. However, the Negro market is receiving more and more consideration from business management and increasing opportunities are being provided for young Negroes to learn to manage service enterprises, especially those which serve predominantly Negro consumers.

An urban future offers expectations, responsibilities, opportunities, and a way of life that is markedly different from that of rural agricultural areas. The future of the Negro child will be one in which he will know all the benefits, critical experiences, and disabilities that belong to the process of urbanization. There will be fewer barriers to change of his status in the city because the very nature of urban life is permissive to shifts in status and roles.

The new citizenship status of Negroes in the South is related to the rearrangement of the Southern population. The relative size of the Negro population sharply declined in the decade 1940–50 and all evidence points to further decline in the period since the 1950 census was taken. Between 1940 and 1950 the Negro population in the South increased

only 1.5 percent. Six Southern states—Alabama, Arkansas,
Georgia, Kentucky, Mississippi, and Oklahoma—had smaller
Negro populations in 1950 than in 1940.

There is evidence that increasing numbers of young Negroes are looking forward to futures in the South rather than
planning to realize their hopes and dreams outside of the
South. Even many young Negroes who go outside the South
for their career preparation expect to follow those careers in
the South. The progress of Negro communities in Durham,
Atlanta, Nashville and New Orleans is evidence of this.
The improvement of living conditions among all classes in
these cities over the past decade bolsters the confidence
that some Negroes have in the future of the South. The success of the small professional and business group of Negroes
and the high standard of living they enjoy is an example
before Negro children today. The gradual growth of the
number of Negro voters and the attention politicians give
their expressed wishes is also an encouragement. Negro children and youth see a future in the South that is emerging
despite the drag of the traditional folkways, which on every
hand show an ability to retard and delay, but in no place to
stay, the future of an urban industrial South where all people
will have fuller enjoyment of the citizenship privileges to
which they are entitled.

Preparing for the Future

Transmission of the culture to the young both through
formal education and informally and preparing the young
for their functions and roles through various social devices

are preparation for the future of the society. But education cannot prepare the young for the future when the future has not been anticipated with a reasonable degree of realism. Sometimes only a crisis will bring about the realization that the education which is being provided falls short of its intended purpose.

Few books have had such an impact on American thinking about a social issue as *The Uneducated* by Eli Ginzberg and Douglas Bray.[6] The facts presented on illiteracy in World War II were little short of astonishing. Because the mental screening by the Armed Services, as the authors say, "was mainly a measure of educational deprivation, the results of the large-scale examinations are helpful in determining the number and distribution of persons who were so educationally deprived that they were considered unsuitable for military service during the most important war in the country's history." Negroes from the Southeast and Southwest accounted for 88 percent of Negro rejections.

The Uneducated provides statistics to draw a picture in which the South may not take pride and the rest of the nation may not take comfort. Of the 716,400 men rejected for mental deficiency, 525,520 were from the South. Identified according to race, 238,260 were white and 287,260 were Negroes. Stated as rejections per 1,000 men registered, the rates were, for the country as a whole: white, 25; Negro, 152. For the states in the Southeast the rates were: white, 52; Negro, 202. The highest rejection rates for Negroes were in South Carolina

---

[6] Eli Ginzberg and Douglas Bray, *The Uneducated* (New York: Columbia University Press, 1953).

with a rate of 277 and Louisiana with a rate of 247. In addition to these rejections the Army actually inducted 384,000 illiterate men: 220,000 white and 164,000 Negro.

It is apparent that both Negroes and whites had educational disadvantages, since the white rate in the South was double that for whites in the nation as a whole, and the Negro rate in the South was one-third greater than the national rate for Negroes.

The lesson of the Selective Service reports is that a large segment of the country's youth lacked minimum literacy needed to assume responsibilities of maturity. The 1954 reports of Selective Service show that in five southern States —Alabama, Georgia, Mississippi, North Carolina, and South Carolina—more than 30 percent of the Selective Service registrants were disqualified on the mental test while none of the Southern states had fewer than 15 percent so disqualified. Outside of the South disqualifications on this test taken at random were: California 9.6, Colorado, 4.8, Pennsylvania 3.7, and Iowa 1.4.

The first real concern, nationally and regionally, about the effective literacy of Negroes came as a result of these rejection rates of Selective Service during World War II. The comparative inferiority of schools for Negroes became a consideration in the desegregation of schools as evidenced by the earnest efforts of Southern public officials to improve Negro schools even if there was no real intent to make them equal to those of whites. Since 1950 there has been accelerated investment in educational facilities for Negroes both at the elementary school and higher levels. Donald

J. Bogue in a paper in *The New South and Higher Education* concluded that "A rise in the average level of educational attainment was one of the greatest of the recent transformations in the South. The level of educational attainment climbed much faster for the South's nonwhite population than for the white. The number of nonwhite Southerners with some high school or college education increased faster than for white Southerners in all geographic divisions." [7]

In the decade 1940–1950 the gap between provision of education for Negroes and whites began to narrow. Expenditures, school plants and facilities, the length of school term, the training of teachers all showed a marked advance. Pressures brought to bear on the South brought this increase in educational provisions. "In November, 1955, *Southern School News* estimated that $2,556,500,000 had been spent or appropriated for new school construction in 16 states and the District of Columbia since 1949." [8]

In the course of ninety years those who controlled educational policy succeeded in erecting a great barrier between the Negro school and the white school in the South. Actually the segregration of schools was a mechanism for admitting some to knowledge while withholding it from others. The discerning in the South were aware of this. The president of a Negro land-grant college, discussing the institution to which he had given many years of service, summed up his

[7] Jessie P. Guzman, ed., *The New South and Higher Education* (Tuskegee Institute, Ala.: The Department of Research and Records, 1954).

[8] Shoemaker et al., *With All Deliberate Speed*, p. 93.

problems in the simple statement that: "The Negro Land-Grant college was designed and operated so as to never teach a Negro anything that would put him in competition with a white man."

Ernest W. Swanson and John A. Griffin make the point that "the out-migration of southern peoples means that the quality of public education in the South, especially that available to the Negro population, has more than academic importance for the nation as a whole and for certain selected non-southern states in particular." [9] To this it might be added that the farm-to-city shift means that the quality of southern rural education is of obvious concern to urban school systems, both South and North.

The numbers of Negro children help make it important. "There can be no doubt that the burden of educating children is much heavier in the South, particularly the rural South, than in the heavily industrialized Northeast. The differences are so great that, although the continuing urbanization of the South and migration out of the South are doubtlessly narrowing the gap, it will long remain. One of the major products of the South is babies. One of its major exports to other parts of the country is young adults." [10]

Negro children today are attending school in greater numbers, starting at earlier ages and remaining in school longer. Negro parents and Negro youth themselves are conscious of the fact they must prepare for a future that is theirs in a

[9] Ernst W. Swanson and John A. Griffin, *Public Education in the South Today and Tomorrow* (Chapel Hill, N.C.: University of North Carolina Press, 1955).

[10] Ginzberg and Bray, *The Uneducated*, pp. 188–89.

sense that other generations of Negroes have not known. This position makes them insistent that they secure the education they believe they need rather than accept an education another group may consider adequate for them.

During the past decade young Negroes have learned more about school from outside experiences than from class instruction. As an institution around which controversy has centered, the public school has come up for reassessment. Negro children now know more about the provisions and operations of public schools than most adults did ten years ago. They have to go through hostile crowds and into classrooms where they are unwelcome. No parent or friend or even advocate can do this for them. They have done it for themselves in Clinton and Little Rock and Charlotte. When Negro teen-agers made these pioneering journeys with television following their progress for other Negro children everywhere to see, the Negro child got another kind of preparation for the future. These children are aware that others may make opportunities possible for them but they alone can take advantage of an opportunity. They must be prepared for this as an unpleasant experience.

The Negro child in the South today has a better understanding of the Supreme Court, the Presidency, and the Congress than foregoing generations had. It is, moreover, an understanding that relates these institutions directly to his fortunes and welfare. Experiences of Negro youth in this decade and their discussion have provided an uncommon education in the value content of American culture, including political principles and processes of the government under which we live. Perhaps no other generation of young people has had so intensive an indoctrination in the American value system and certainly none has had the inconsistencies and contradictions so clearly presented to it. Southern children and youth have had conflicting social expectations defined for them and negations of these expectations spelled out in detail. No other generation of the young has been so confronted with the bright illusions of our political institutions or has had these illusions so ruthlessly attacked.

Final decision has not been left to legislators, public officials, or the courts. Various sorts of pressure and propaganda groups have debated the status of the Negro child now and in the future. Most adhere to nonviolent aims and methods. The championing organizations, particularly the NAACP, have been publicized, and power and influence far greater than they possess have been attributed to them. This has certainly impressed the Negro child. Negro children have learned how pressure groups are organized and the strategies and tactics they use. They are observing means that may be used to effect social and political actions as well as techniques to prevent and obstruct these by an organized minority. How they use these skills in social manipulation remains to be seen. Lessons in direct social action in subversion and in thwarting the popular will provide tools for use for ill as well as for good.

The waves of migration from the rural South to cities within and without have always brought problems. The migrants are responsible for unduly high proportions of crime, delinquency, and dependency in the cities to which they go. Despite the repetition of these circumstances over many years, no program has been developed to prepare people for migration in the places from which they go. Nor has there been a program to prepare people for adjustment in the places to which they come. This results in tremendous human waste as well as consumption of public revenue to care for those ill-adapted to urban living. Negro children have an intimate acquaintance with these social problems because many of them were not prepared for the new circumstances they face.

Negro children have learned that some action for the common welfare must be taken by the federal government and that those who argue most loudly for states rights leave undone vitally important social tasks. They know how remiss local government can be in providing for public services, for security of the person, and for enjoyment of citizenship rights. Their preparation for the future includes an expectation that the federal government can do and will do certain social tasks made essential by the magnitude of their problems.

Self-Image

The experiences of Negro children in the South during the past decade might well be expected to have affected their conceptions of themselves. Their behavior and conduct offer evidence of some attributes of their self-image. Their self-esteem ranges from pride to bumptiousness. Ideas they hold about their opportunities are expressed in striving to realize an ambition by some and demand for unearned rewards by others. Consciousness of having powerful and influential advocates of their greater opportunity is expressed in quiet confidence by some and a challenging arrogance by others. Encouragement to venture where their parents did not dare has affected the respect shown for parents and teachers who urge caution and restraint. As in all revolutionary circumstances in which a new freedom is gained there is considerable aimless, random, irresponsible behavior on the part of those who have no constructive goals. Uncertainty and a sense of inadequacy are revealed in a truculence that challenges any imposed discipline.

The one clear feature of the new self-image of Negro youth of whatever status is a sense of security expressed by assuming positive and sometimes aggressive attitudes and postures. A Southern white man who recently returned to the South after eight years in other parts of the world said that the most startling change he noticed was that "Negroes look you straight in the eye now." The newly-gained confidence that young Negroes have in themselves and their feeling of security in expressing their aspirations appear to be disturbing facts of contemporary Southern life that many Southern white people are loath to face.

The cherished illusion of Southern whites that Negroes were "satisfied" with their status and opportunities—"their place"—is being clung to despite accumulation of a mass of contrary evidence. During the decade a governor of Mississippi was positively flabbergasted when a conference of Negro educators called by him with full confidence that they would support his program for voluntary segregation refused to do so.

Charles S. Johnson wrote in 1956 what would become the valedictory to his long career of studying race relations. He said: "The present-day Southern Negro does not share the belief of the Southern white that he is inferior as a human being, even though he may earn lower wages and have fewer years of schooling. . . . What is for white Southerners most difficult to understand, in these days, is the absence of both the belief in inferiority and the simulation of this belief. The Southern Negro viewpoint is more broadly national than regional. There are very few, if any, Southern Negroes who do not want full American citizenship, even though there are undoubtedly those who, if they had it, would make no better use of it than some of their white counterparts. In philosophy the Southern Negro identification is with the nation and not with the Southern region, which is, in spirit, separatist." [11]

Negro youth strive to give the impression of not feeling inferior even if the behavior of some is clear evidence that they are over-compensating for such feeling. Unfortunately, a type of juvenile delinquency among Negro children and youth is appearing in the South. It is expressed in challenges to the traditional authority of whiteness and to that of Negro adults who occupy their positions through white authority.

Perhaps the most unfortunate aspect of the young Negro's conception of himself is that he must depend upon himself

[11] The New York *Times* Magazine, September 23, 1956.

to carry his battle with the support of few, if any, white people in his local community. Those whites who are sympathetic to his cause are silent for very good reasons of their own. Those who most loudly declare their "friendship" for him are those who do so confidently asserting they know no "good" Negro has aspirations of equality, and who denounce his heroes and threaten mayhem if he persists in pursuit of his ambitions. A state official in high office expressed this often repeated opinion: "I'm the best friend the Negro ever had but integration will come only over my dead body." If such are the Negro's white "friends," no wonder he is convinced he has none. It is certainly unfortunate when Negro youth get the idea that they must protect themselves or be prepared to do so because the duly constituted authority for preserving the security of citizens in their home communities leaves them at the mercy of enemies who would do violence to them. While their elders are cautioning them to turn the other cheek, many come to feel that their security lies in their readiness to meet violence with violence.

Another feature of the new self-image is that young Negroes are seeing themselves as leaders rather than as being in preparation for leadership. Students who suffered indignities as the first ones to enter desegregated schools, with the responsibility for persisting in their attendance despite discouraging experiences, feel this way. Students who challenged bus segregation in Tallahassee, those who staged a boycott in Orangeburg, and those who mounted a campaign to desegregate business establishments in Oklahoma have some of the feeling. The problem growing out of such a self-conception is the danger of intemperate actions that may draw reprisals.

A third feature of the new self-image is that young Negroes do not feel themselves to be a helpless minority. Instead they consider the die-hard segregationists, whatever their positions may be in the community or however important may be the political offices they hold, to be the minority. And they scoff at them as ludicrous buffoons clinging desperately to a lost cause. The young Negro in the South sees himself as belonging to the majority that includes the federal government, Negroes who have advanced outside the South, and white people of powerful influence outside the South. Problems posed by this feature of the new self-image are: 1) raising an obstruction to an early rapprochement with young Southern whites, and 2) the disenchantment possible if their allies give them too little or too tardy support.

A fourth feature of the new self-image is the belief that they hold to the great human values uncompromisingly. This is especially true in relating their struggle to the independence struggles of Asia and Africa. A problem raised by this conception is the possibility that some may join the divisive black nationalist movements in the United States, which would be a rejection of all the arduous struggle for integration and would bring further tension and conflict.

The major question the Negro youth's new self-image raises is what positive approaches can be taken in order that a constructive productive humanism can mature out of the current personality conflicts in a setting of social confusion.

SPANISH-SPEAKING CHILDREN

by JOHN H. BURMA

CHILDREN from Spanish-speaking backgrounds are very much like any other children, and, basically, their problems are the same as those of ordinary Anglo-American children, with the significant addition of acculturation, culture conflict, and assimilation. These latter may be significantly out of proportion, for they may lead to difficulties which otherwise would not have arisen or would not have been as acute.

In this discussion no inviolately rigorous use of the terms Mexican, Mexican American, or Spanish-speaking people is feasible, because of the confused use of these terms by the general public. Therefore, the noun "Mexican" will be used to mean a native of Mexico, usually an adult; the term "Mexican American" will mean a native-born citizen of Mexican ancestry, a naturalized citizen, or a child who emigrated from Mexico early in his life. "Spanish-speaking

John H. Burma is Chairman of the Department of Sociology at Grinnell College.
Considerable use is made throughout this chapter of data in John H. Burma, *Spanish-Speaking Groups in the United States* (Durham: Duke University Press, 1954), without footnoting or other special reference.

people" is used to refer inclusively to Mexicans, Mexican Americans, Puerto Ricans, and Spanish Americans. Where the group is mixed, the attempt is to designate it according to the majority of the members.

The Mexican American Child

There are in the United States today approximately 3.5 million people of Mexican origin or ancestry (the census makes no exact count), of whom possibly 1.5 million are children and youth. This large number of Mexican American youth exists because Mexicans have been likely to emigrate as families, and because of the relatively high birth rate of Mexican families. Mexican immigration was only a trickle until about 1915, but large numbers came between then and 1930. From 1930 to 1940 this flow reversed itself to emigration, but turned again after 1940 and has continued strong for twenty years. The majority of adults in this group were born in Mexico, but the majority of youth were born in the United States.

Approximately 40 percent of Mexican American youth live in Texas, another 40 percent in California, and the remainder in Colorado, Arizona, New Mexico, Illinois, Kansas, Michigan, New York—in fact, in almost every state. In numerous school districts of Texas, California, and New Mexico, Spanish-speaking children make up one-fourth or more of the total students. As a rule there exist social and residential segregation wherever there are large numbers of Mexican Americans, although where their number is small, there usually is little or no segregation. Throughout Texas,

California, and the other states with large Mexican American population, the Mexican American child suffers a special and serious handicap in becoming a successful American citizen as the result of being segregated by Anglos and of segregating himself from Anglos. It is the child growing up under these conditions with whom we are here most concerned, whether he lives in rural Texas or the slums of New York City. A relatively small proportion of Spanish-speaking children are from Puerto Rico; these will be discussed at the end of this chapter.

FAMILY AND HOME. As with all children, the family of the Mexican American child is of great importance in his development. Historically the Mexican family has been of the extended type, including grandparents, uncles and aunts, and cousins. This has the effect of giving the child a wide circle from whom he may receive emotional support, warmth of acceptance, stability, and a real feeling of belonging. These contributions are much to be desired (and have been suggested as probable factors in the lower rate of psychoses found among Mexican Americans). In this sense it is unfortunate that the extended family system runs counter to the American middle-class nuclear family pattern, hampers acculturation and assimilation, and tends to limit the individual largely to contacts with family members. These are serious handicaps for a child who is marginal (i.e., living on edges of two cultures but wholly in neither), and has contributed to the retention of the "colony" (*colonia*) housing pattern among Mexican Americans. The extended family and the *colonia* help explain why most Mexican American children have few if any Anglo friends. In the past, most recreation was found in the home and most free time was spent in the home; this is still true, but is observably decreasing. The extended family pattern is itself in a state of decline; the third generation does not want it as a day-to-day relationship, but only as a matter of frequent family get-togethers.

Other changes are occurring in behavior and attitudes toward matters relating to the family. Families plan for, and have, fewer children. The role of godparents in the life of the child is becoming negligible. There is an increasing desire by the Mexican American to function as an individual rather than as a subordinate unit in an extended family structure. This leads to "unfilial" behavior, and some consequent misunderstanding and estrangement between generations. This may become particularly acute before the marriage of the children, for under the extended family system marriage is a matter of group concern and activity; under the nucleated family system marriage is a private concern.

As acculturation increases there are changes in family roles. The father becomes less dominant, and shows more affection for the wife and children; the wife is less subordinate as the result of mutual sharing of authority and discipline; the education of the wife equals or surpasses that of the husband; the possibility of the wife working outside the home is looked upon with more favor. The gap between the freedom permitted boys and girls, although still great, is decreasing; girls are less strictly supervised, but still are more closely watched than are boys; supervision of both is least among the lower class. "Nice" girls are now permitted more dating than previously—which was almost nil—but still much less than Anglo girls. In most of these matters class differences are quite observable, with the lower and upper classes, for different reasons, most closely approaching the Anglo norm; the middle class is slowest to change, seeming to feel that their prized "family respectability" requires the perpetuation of the older attitudes and behavior patterns.

Sometimes an additional cleavage between generations results when parents who cling tenaciously to the old culture have children who seek rapid, complete assimilation. This not only causes heartache, but may leave the second generation without adequate adult models or adult guidance, and foster the formation of gangs, whose influence on the child and control of his behavior then are greater than they normally would be.

Important to any family is the home and the neighborhood in which it lives. Almost always in the Southwest, and commonly elsewhere, the Mexican immigrant lives in a segregated subcommunity. By whatever name is it known, this area is substandard and its reputation, among Anglos, is not a savory one. Nearly all these *colonias* are below the average of their parent city in such things as size and quality of housing, electricity, inside toilets, and piped hot water. The families of migratory agricultural workers have a poorer situation, for in the spring they leave their shacks for the even worse housing available to migatory laborers. Here and there public housing projects have been provided to improve this situation, but probably two-thirds to three-fourths of all Mexican American children live in substandard houses located in substandard communities. The lighter, the more well-to-do, and the more assimilated he and his parents are, the less the discrimination and the less likely he is to live in such an area.

EDUCATION. The educational opportunities and activities of any child are of great significance; this is especially true if he is the child of immigrant parents coming from a country of low average education and entering a country of high average education. Adult Mexican immigrants brought with them an average of about five years of formal education, the attitude that neither sex, particularly girls, needed a high-school education, and little belief in the general value of education for anyone except well-to-do and professional people.

Thus the chief problem relating to the education of Mexican American children before 1930 was that of getting them into school. This problem was solved with reasonable success, but there next arose the problem of segregated schools. In many areas in Texas, California, and some other parts of the Southwest, Mexican American children were required to attend segregated schools or were placed in segregated classrooms. As usual, "segregated" meant second class or worse, and from the 1930s to the middle '40s the removal of these barriers was a major concern. During the 1946–48 period, various federal courts ruled against this segregation, and in the succeeding dozen years desegregation has become almost complete. Segregation sometimes still exists through gerrymandering and the fact that schools near Mexican subcommunities are likely to be labeled "Mexican" schools and hence shunned by Anglos.

Today the chief problem is early dropout of Mexican

American students. Enrollments are good in the primary grades but then decline so that by high school they probably average no more than half the potential. Low income is a serious barrier, and since many of these parents have had little formal education they are not successful in explaining to their children why they should graduate from high school —if indeed the parents see this as desirable.

Part of the explanation for this problem also is to be found in the fact that Mexican American pupils typically are over-age for their grade placement. Either they have missed school to follow the crops, or their language handicaps have been too severe, or they started late and always have been overage. In some cases, as the child reaches adolescence the disparity between his age and that of his schoolmates is magnified for him and is a significant factor in his lack of desire to remain in school. In others, behavior which would be normal two grades ahead is viewed as alarmingly precocious by Anglo mothers who do not take into account the normal significant differences between the behavior of a twelve-year-old girl and that of a fourteen-year-old girl, even if they happen to share the same school room.

From the standpoint of the children themselves, probably their chief educational problem is their linguistic handicap. The normal educational procedure is to admit children to school at six or seven, carry on all teaching in English, and trust that they will learn the language and the content material simultaneously. This does occur under optimum conditions; i.e., when the child is bright, strongly motivated and encouraged, sympathetically taught, and wholeheartedly included by his classmates in all activities. Unfortunately such a situation is rather rare, and most commonly the child learns both language and content imperfectly. Often this language handicap, difficult at any time, becomes progressively worse until it becomes insurmountable and the child fails repeatedly and finally leaves school.

This linguistic difficulty of Mexican American pupils was used as a rationalization by those who wished educational segregation for social reasons. It was stated that segregation gave the Spanish-speaking student a "language benefit." Today professional opinion is virtually unanimous that the best way to teach English is to place the child in a class where most of the children speak English.

Another educational problem, much less dramatic than language, but equally significant, is the average Mexican American child's relatively low economic, social, and cultural level. These factors are serious handicaps for any child, and the superimposition on them of bi-lingualism, cultural conflicts, and assimilation problems often has unfortunate results. Teachers report occupational orientation and health education as problems frequently encountered. Some of the more alert school systems report considerable difficulty in presenting the Mexican cultural heritage adequately either to the majority or minority groups. Certainly an indispensable element in a complete school program for mixed schools must be the education of Anglo children to some appreciation of the Mexican culture. Most states with large numbers of Mexican American students now publish guides to aid teachers with Spanish-speaking students.

In addition to these difficulties, a significant number of Mexican American children must move about with their parents who are engaged in migratory agricultural labor. This means at best shifting schools several times, and at worst attending school only a few months of the year. Under a situation of permanent or temporary mobility the child and his parents must value education very highly to make the necessary effort and sacrifices so that the child can attend school regularly. Various educational experiments have been tried in coping with the migrant child, but none has been outstandingly successful, so the great bulk of such children attend regular community schools. Here they create problems. Sometimes they cause serious, if temporary, overcrowding. They present a difficult challenge to teachers to provide a program which has meaning and value for them, permits them to learn at their own level and pace, and which takes into account their special needs without jeopardizing the program of the permanent pupil. The best solution, a highly flexible, individualistic learning program, is good for the permanent children as well as the migrants, but unfortunately, such a program is difficult to organize and staff, and expensive to maintain.

To be successful in such a program, a school must plan an adequate method. This may be done by a "big brother" system, by a class room host and hostess, by special use of Spanish-speaking permanent students, and by practical study units on cotton, vegetables, beets, purchasing, health, family living—and Mexico. The school must have available class materials on a wide range of levels, so the migrant child may begin where he is fitted to begin and may receive individual assistance as he needs it. Account must be taken of bilingualism by emphasizing the use of oral English, yet protecting the child with a limited knowledge of the language; respect should be shown for Spanish, and at least a smattering of it should be taught to Anglo children.

In general, the educational picture for Mexican American children is a constantly brightening one. Segregation is disappearing, and schools and teachers are better equipped and more deeply motivated to handle special problems. Mexican American standards of living are improving and migratory labor is decreasing. A rapidly increasing number of pupils are children of native-born parents and bring to school a considerable knowledge of American customs and language. In short, at the chief points of tension the strain is gradually lessening, and at the same time better techniques for dealing with these problems are being developed and more widely used.

DELINQUENCY. Wherever there are sizable numbers of Mexican American youth, they have the reputation of being more delinquency-prone than Anglo youth. Although this is likely to be exaggerated, it does exist. Delinquency is related in some way to a number of factors: living in slum or substandard areas, employment of both parents away from home, educational difficulties, association with persons who break the law, low family income, poor recreation, the power of the gang, lack of occupational opportunity, lack of strict supervision, culture conflict, movement from rural to urban areas, family disorganization. All these impinge upon the average Mexican American youth more than the average Anglo youth, and hence we predict and find a higher delinquency rate among Mexican Americans. For example, most youth are rather strongly motivated to make money, to be liked, and to "be somebody." There are many avenues to achieve these goals and most of them are socially acceptable. A high proportion of the socially approved avenues are virtually closed, however, to Mexican American youth, while none of the socially disapproved avenues are closed. Thus the chances of the Mexican American youth choosing one of the disapproved methods of goal-seeking are greater than they are for the average Anglo boy—through no fault of his own but because of societal factors over which he has no control.

For all immigrants and their children, cultural differences or culture conflict are potential sources of disorganization, and this is true for Mexican Americans. For example, in Mexico it is normal for men and boys to idle on the street corner in the evening, amusing themselves and getting the day's news. In this country if boys spend much time loafing on the streets in the evenings they are likely to get into trouble with the law. Moreover, in Mexico the pattern was to release the boy from most parental controls when he was around sixteen, so that he might "become a man"; this usually meant sex, gambling, alcohol, and potentially some fighting. It was assumed that the boy would have his fling for a year or two, get it out of his system, and marry and settle down to become a respectable adult. In the United States if this kind of release occurs at the same age, the boy is only half through high school, and may be four to six years away from settling down as an adult. Here he is considered a delinquent and may be sent to a training school.

In the past fifteen years the spotlight has been on Mexican American gangs as products and producers of delinquency. From San Antonio to Los Angeles these youngsters are called *pachucos*, or simply *'chucs*, and are looked down upon by Anglos and by some Mexican Americans. Usually they are marginal persons, lost between the old Mexican world which they do not accept and the new American world which does not accept them. The core of the *pachuco* world is the neighborhood gang, not the home or school, and the members of the gang feel for it a great attachment. Their rejection of parts of the Mexican culture is closely related to the cleavage between this age group and the parent group. It is particularly unfortunate that the isolation from the parent group usually occurs before the youngsters have achieved access to Anglo society. Whenever this type of situation occurs, teen-aged gangs are strong and prevalent. Their members go out of their way to make themselves visible and to demonstrate "belonging," by ducktail and fender haircuts, special clothes, whiskers, sunglasses ("shades"), self-tattoos, and a special language, *pachucana*—part Spanish, part English, part jive, part manufactured or invented. Not all Mexican American youth who sport some of these external characteristics are actual *pachucos*; for many of them the true *pachucos* are just a reference group, one to which they feel some psychic kinship, or to which they aspire eventually, but with which they presently have no direction connection.

Group workers and probation officers say most *pachucos* are not antisocial, but are so painfully social that they are willing to make great sacrifices to achieve acceptance, status, and "belonging." The strength, uniqueness, and social cohesion of these groups undoubtedly are increased by language and cultural factors.

It must not be assumed from the foregoing paragraphs that there is a wholesale revolt among Mexican American youth against their parents. This is far from true, and the situation is a great deal more complex than such an oversimplification might indicate. Both parents and children agree on the desirability of rapid assimilation and uphold many of the attitudes and goals of Anglo culture. In such families the parents may speak only English to their children, and both may be motivated strongly toward education and upward mobility. They may seek Anglo friends, residence outside the *colonia,* and Anglo jobs. In school these children tend to achieve better than the average, to be liked by their teachers, and to find some small acceptance by the Anglo students.

The attitudes of other Mexican American youth toward this group of "squares" range from acceptance, jealousy, and grudging emulation on one extreme to almost hate on the other. Many *pachucos,* however, retain much *Mexicanissmo* and indicate great pride in their parents' cultural heritage. Anyone who turns his back on this heritage (speaking English only, for example) may be termed a *falso,* is thought to consider himself "too good for the rest of us," and may expect to be roughed up occasionally if he lives in a *pachuco* neighborhood. In actuality the great majority of Mexican American youth fall between the "squares" and the *pachucos* on the continuum. They seek assimilation, but not avidly, and retain, partly by inertia, a considerable amount of the old culture. They attend school dutifully, if without much enthusiasm, and have hopes (realistic or not) of finishing high school and getting a "good" job. Only for the "square" group is there any hope of attending college. Members of the great middle group may engage in delinquent acts, but their frequency and seriousness are likely to be considerably less than are those of the true delinquent. Obviously it is this middle group who offer the greatest hope and challenge to concerned agencies and individuals. This group has all kinds of problems, but most of them are not insurmountable in size or of such depth that they cannot be alleviated by known, normal means.

CULTURE. Of the various problems faced by Mexican American youth, none are more clearly different from those of Anglo youth than the ones related to acculturation, assimilation, culture conflict, and marginality. In the United States we tend to pay lip service to the concept of cultural pluralism—numerous separate cultures coexisting in cooperative harmony—but in actual practice most Americans tacitly expect cultural conformity and look down upon anyone whose language, color, or ways of life differ from the majority norm. This leads to pressure on any culturally different group to acculturate and to become assimilated.

Some immigrants to America fled from their homeland or in other ways forever severed their ties with the old country.

For them and their children, acquisition of the new culture
was the only possibility they saw for a secure future. Such
motivation has not been strong for all groups; some (Chinese, Italians, Mexicans, etc.) have contained many individuals who looked upon themselves as temporary residents
and who anticipated a return to the homeland within a few
years. For such persons a transfer of loyalty would be both
undesirable and impractical. Elements of the new culture
were accepted or rejected in terms of utility only, and any
which were in serious conflict with the old culture would
not be accepted; the less change and adjustment necessary,
the better.

Many Mexican immigrants entered the United States
with the full intention of returning to Mexico. Men brought
their families with them not because they intended to "settle"
but to keep the family unit intact during their sojourn. They
and their children were Mexicans and intended to remain
so. Under these circumstances acculturation has little utility
and would have negative effects if carried too far.

Immigrants from across the seas had to accumulate a great
deal of money before renewing their family and cultural ties
by a visit to the "old country"; not so with the Mexican immigrant who may return to Mexico easily. Thus the accessi-
bility of Mexico has hindered among Mexican Americans the
acculturation to be found in other groups. Yet some Mexican
immigrants intended from the first to become American
citizens, to live here the rest of their lives, and have expected
their children to do the same. These persons consciously
have sought acculturation and have achieved it as rapidly as

any other group. Thus second generation Mexican American children come from homes which represent both a wide range of attitudes toward acculturation and a wide range of actual acculturation. When the parents, through intent, inertia, or ignorance, cling to the old culture, and the children are sent to a public school which endeavors to inculcate in them middle-class Anglo attitudes, values, and culture patterns, misunderstanding and conflict at home and at school are almost inevitable.

It has been observed that there are three cultures with which the Mexican American child is concerned: the Anglo, the Mexican, and the Mexican-American. The Mexican-American culture often acts as a bridge for the immigrant child; he can acquire it much more easily than the Anglo culture. In general, the Mexican-American culture contains large portions of Anglo material culture and Anglo mass culture, and large portions of Mexican nonmaterial culture. The second generation boy usually has accepted much Anglo material culture, i.e., he understands and wants a bicycle, air rifle, and comic books. As a participant in our mass culture he may play Tarzan, be able to give you the batting average of Mickey Mantle, or be a rock-'n-roll addict. The material culture and mass culture are wide but shallow; the child's real problems come with the more fundamental, ethical, and value aspects of nonmaterial culture, for it is here that serious confusion or conflict occurs.

The public school, which is by far the chief acculturative agency for Mexican American children, usually teaches Anglo middle-class attitudes, values, and norms as if they were

Absolute Truth; to the extent that the school is successful, the child accepts these and either drops or refuses to adopt many of the attitudes, values, and norms presented by his family. Granted complete good will within the family, which is as unrealistic an assumption as it would be among Anglo families, conflict in these matters is inevitable. Hence the typical Mexican American youth of the second or third generation is marginal; this marginality is an anomalous condition, likely to lead to misunderstanding, frustration, and disorganization. Fortunately marginality is dynamic rather than static, and tends to reach a peak and then decline to a less disorganizing level. It is the child who is half-and-half, rather than 10 percent and 90 percent, who suffers most from marginality.

Some of the social disorganization found among marginal Mexican Americans results because such youth have freed themselves from creeds, beliefs, and other social controls which operate within the framework of the old culture, and yet have not acquired wholly the folkways, mores, and social controls of the new Anglo culture. Thus they may suffer from *anomie*, be relatively free from self-discipline or value internalization, and be more easily influenced by matters of the moment. Aimless or delinquent behavior are the frequent results, although strong, disciplined men, dreamers and reformers, as well as hoodlums, alcoholics, and criminals have come from such environments.

Marginality of children may be prolonged by parents who wish to have "the best of both cultures." At first glance this is a laudable goal; in practice it frequently works out unsatisfactorily. Basic to the failure of any such goal is the fact that cultures do not consist of many unrelated bits and pieces, but rather are a weblike, organic whole. Bits may not be abstracted from the whole with impunity, even if other bits arbitrarily are put into place. Thus it appears necessary for the Mexican American to make up his mind which culture he wishes for his own, rather than to drag on, willy-nilly, with unrelated parts of each.

A good illustration is bilingualism; for no one would argue that it is undesirable to know more than one language. Mexican American youngsters are not really taught Spanish, and commonly they read it very imperfectly, write it phonetically and incorrectly, and speak with poor grammar, construction, and vocabulary; and if they take academic Spanish in high school they meet with little more success than they do in English courses. Since such children as a rule also know English imperfectly, they have a mastery of no language. An increasing number of ambitious second generation persons who now are parents do not teach their children Spanish in the home; they fear the child will learn neither language well, and if a choice must be made, they prefer English.

Certainly conflicting values of the two or three cultures with which the Mexican American child has contact is a disorienting factor for him. Neither the Mexican nor the American culture has truly systematic values; each has some contradictory elements. Confusion of values is serious enough to warrant considerable attention by philosophers, social psychologists, educators, and psychiatrists, when only one culture is involved; how much more serious it is when the child is expected to grope toward a workable, acceptable pattern within the maze of two such cultures! That he confronts frustration, confusion, misconception, and disorganization is to be accepted as a matter of course at the same time it is greatly deplored.

The Puerto Rican Child

The second largest group of Spanish-speaking children in America today are the Puerto Ricans. Twenty years ago there were only a few scattered thousands on the mainland, and few of them were children. In 1955 there were between one-half to two-thirds of a million here (despite wild estimates of "millions"), with an estimated 80 percent of the total in New York City alone, including 40,000 to 50,000 children enrolled in the New York City schools. There, in Chicago, and in most major cities between, are found sizable numbers of Puerto Rican youth. Like other immigrant groups of the past, Puerto Ricans are poor, uneducated, lack occupational skills, have little facility with the English language, suffer disproportionately from social problems, and live in the least desirable sections of the city with their high delinquency rates, in part because of discrimination, segregation, and exploitation. Puerto Rican children and youth have serious enough problems to warrant our attention. Except that a higher proportion of Puerto Rican youth are themselves immigrants, and that they are concentrated much more heavily in large urban areas, the situations and problems of Puerto Rican and Mexican American youth are in many respects similar.

Like the Mexican family the Puerto Rican family undergoes changes with immigration. The father's authority over the wife and children declines, freedom of wife and children increases, and for the children freedom sometimes becomes license and incorrigibility. With this group, too, there is likely to be a hiatus between generations which increases misunderstanding and conflict; in part this is the result of the greater acculturation of the child and his consequent marginality, confusion, and disorientation of values and norms. As is so common and so tragic in such cases, usually parents and children each sincerely believe that they are right and the other wrong. Many Puerto Rican women work outside the home, because there is need for additional income or because there is no male breadwinner. This means children too frequently are without the mothers' care during the day, are left with neighbors or in day nurseries, or wait on the streets after school until the parent returns.

The environment of large numbers of Puerto Rican children in the New York City and Chicago school systems has caused more problems than one would expect, because of the attempt to put into practice new educational philosophies. Instead of the older rapid assimilation philosophy, the new philosophy maintains that the cultural and social contributions which Puerto Ricans and other groups can make should be utilized; that education for all children need not mean the same education for all children, but rather individualized instruction, assistance, and remedial work geared to the needs and interests of each child; and that teaching should encompass the total development of the individual for his best total adjustment. These philosophies and goals, although highly desirable, do create extra problems whenever large numbers of youngsters as different as the Puerto Rican children enter a school system. Inevitably the school to which the Puerto Rican child is assigned is much different from the one with which he or his parents were familiar in Puerto Rico, and many of the values and norms peripheral to education are different (such as participation of girls in after-school programs), so that tri-cornered misunderstandings between parent, school, and child easily arise, but are not so easily resolved.

Some of the techniques which have been evolved to meet these problems in New York City include the use of Spanish-speaking interpreters at registration time and other methods of making the parents and child feel accepted, booklets in Spanish to explain the school's aims and rules, the use of a buddy or big brother system, assignment to orientation or vestibule classes where emphasis is placed on remedial and language arts work and from which the student is moved when he is ready, a conscious attempt to involve parents as much as possible in school activities and interests, and the use of special Spanish-speaking guidance counsellors.

Unlike the Mexican Americans, Puerto Ricans never have been subjected to educational segregation, but the quality of the school systems from which the immigrant children come is such that they usually are retarded a year or more. The fact that these young people have special needs for vocational training, health, and hygiene, and community awareness makes their satisfactory education even more difficult. Almost without exception Puerto Rican students have serious linguistic handicaps, despite the fact that immigrant children have been taught some English in the Puerto Rican schools.

One of the most frustrating aspects of mainland living for many immigrant Puerto Rican children is our color bar. On the island three groups are recognized: the white, the Negro, and the *grifo*, who is mixed; there is not much discrimination against the Negro, and almost none against the *grifo* except socially; the *grifo* thinks of himself as somewhat above the Negro. When a *grifo* comes to the mainland, he finds himself not only classed as a Negro, which threatens his status, but also subjected to far more discrimination than was directed against the Negro on his home island. The results may be confusion, bitterness, frustration, aggression, or a "don't care" or "what's the use" attitude. By mainland standards from a third to a half of Puerto Ricans are colored —considerably more than by island standards. The Puerto Rican mulatto child is not only subjected to discrimination on the mainland, he faces difficulty in thinking of himself as originally Puerto Rican and Spanish, since he is looked upon by most people as a Negro. His problem of self-evaluation and self-concept may lead to psychic disturbance. Certainly this is one reason for Puerto Rican gang membership; in the gang he is accepted for what he is, stands on his own merit, and has security.

In general the problems of the Puerto Rican child are basically those which most of our immigrants have faced and overcome in the past: language handicaps, overcrowded housing in slum and delinquency areas, poverty and all its secondary aspects, discrimination and low status, educational difficulties, recreational inadequacy, and the problems of acculturation, assimilation, and culture conflict. The historic pattern on the East Coast has been for the immigrant group to settle in an ethnic slum area and there to reproduce for a generation the culture patterns of the old country. The younger people gradually move away to undifferentiated housing areas until the ethnic area, as an area, no longer exists. The "white" Puerto Ricans are following this traditional pattern, and the social world of the Negro Puerto Ricans, at first bounded by the apartment house and the street, expands more slowly. This change comes more easily for those who live outside the New York City area. The assimilation of Puerto Rican youth is hindered in New York by the absence of concrete, homogeneous norms to which to adjust. The kaleidoscope pattern of New York City produces neither a clear norm to which to conform nor the social controls conducive to conformity which may be found elsewhere. Lack of homogeneity of behavior, however, is not always a serious handicap in a heterogeneous social world.

Coming late, as they do, in our stream of immigrants, Puerto Rican children benefit from the wisdom gained by trial-and-error techniques used on other groups. Metropolitan schools and social agencies know better how to handle such problems than before. The Puerto Rican immigrant child brings with him knowledge of some elements of American mass culture acquired in Puerto Rico, and at least some knowledge of the language on which to build. He already is a citizen, and suffers little more from divided loyalty than does a transplanted Texan. For a significant number, their color will be a serious handicap from their school days forward. In short, Puerto Rican children suffer all the handicaps of any children living under comparable socio-economic conditions, plus special problems which are cultural and racial in nature; yet they have better and more sympathetic assistance in meeting all these problems than any previous group on the East Coast. There is every reason to believe that their problems will decline in the future.

The Spanish American Child

Although relatively fewer in number, the problems and prospects of Spanish American children also are of importance. There are in New Mexico several tens of thousands of Spanish American children. Although they are tenth generation native American, this group until a generation ago had clung tenaciously to its own variation of Spanish culture, and hence its children have most of the problems of Mexican American or Puerto Rican children, at least in terms of cultural differences. They suffer a mixture of ethnic and class discrimination, but not in overwhelming degree. They, too, must choose which culture to follow, and consequently are typically marginal, with all that this implies. On the other hand, many of them live in stable families in their own small agricultural communities, or in cities like Albuquerque and Santa Fe where their numbers are so great that they do not feel isolated.

Like other Spanish-speaking children their greatest handicap, other than poverty and its secondary results, is their language difficulty in school, which results in an average achievement less than that of Anglo children. Spanish Americans are a proud group, but this has not prevented many adolescent boys from needing the psychic security received from gang membership, and so-called *pachucos* are as common in cities in New Mexico as in California or Texas.

Although these children are now and for some time in the future will be handicapped by poverty, lack of economic opportunity, linguistic inadequacy, marginality, and culture conflict, their opportunities and outlook seem at least as good as those of Mexican American or Puerto Rican youth.

JUVENILE DELINQUENCY

by ROBERT M. MAC IVER

"PARENTAGE," Bernard Shaw wrote, "is a very important profession, but no test of fitness is ever imposed in the interests of the children." None the less the great majority of parents succeed, somehow or other, under all sorts of conditions and often in the face of considerable handicaps, in bringing up their children to become at least as good citizens as they are themselves. And sometimes it happens that parents of high standards have children who deviate into delinquency. There are no universals here to guide our search for cause or cure. But a growing consensus of research findings indicates that the parting of the ways, the redirection of the child toward habits of antisocial behavior, begins very frequently in the stresses and strains of parent-child relationships.

We must not, however, interpret this conclusion too narrowly. The family is not an island apart from the group and the neighborhood. Tensions aroused within it may be in-

Robert M. MacIver is Director of the Juvenile Delinquency Evaluation Project of New York City and Professor Emeritus of Sociology and Political Philosophy at Columbia University.

duced by the forces that bear on it. Parent or child or both may be so disturbed by outside influences, by the social or economic conditions to which they are exposed, that the relation between the two deteriorates. To take one of many cases, if the child is retarded educationally and has consequent troubles and frustrations in his schooling, he resorts to truancy. The father, worried by this or by the school investigator, rough-handles him, not knowing any better, and the process of alienation between home and school sets in. We should not assume that the children of families in the higher-delinquency areas are inherently more prone to misbehavior than more favored children, nor is parental failure by any means always a sufficient explanation. The lack of outlets for youthful energies, the cultural deprivation of the home, the congestion of living space, the paucity of opportunities and incentives that others enjoy, and not infrequently a sense of being discriminated against, these and other adverse influences corrode the attitudes of the young, while the parents in turn suffer from like frustrations.

Human beings, and not least children, have a remarkable capacity for surmounting unfavorable conditions. Even under the conditions suggested above the large majority of children grow up to be respectable law-abiding citizens. But with some, either the stresses are greater or the natural disposition is less resistant, and these, chafing at restraints and unable to solve their problems, become disoriented in their society and most often alienated at home, with father or mother or both. Some of them are brought up in "broken" homes, but more of them in emotionally "broken" homes, where often lack of guidance, lack of reasonable discipline, or the sheer lack of understanding between the older and the younger generation confirms the process that ends in the hardened delinquent who finds his only congenial society in the company and under the code of the underworld.

If then we hold that juvenile delinquency is a problem that has its focus within the family, we do not thereby assign full responsibility for it to the family itself, and we do not imply that either therapy or prevention depends only on methods that might be brought to bear within the family circle. The emotional tone of family life is a composite of various factors. Rarely do we find a culture group so enclaved within its own traditions that family standards are sheltered from such impacts. This is the case, for example, with the Chinese colony in lower Manhattan, where, incidentally, we find a complete absence of the juvenile delinquency characteristic of congested city areas. In like manner certain religious groups anchored in a highly distinctive orthodoxy are in degree immunized from social influences and trends.

Socio-Economic Factors

The importance of the socio-economic factors, as they react on family life, must be grasped if we are to interpret the incidence of delinquency or are concerned with remedial policies. Under socio-economic factors we include particularly the complex consisting of low economic level, deteriorated and overcrowded housing, lack of training or experience for the competitive urban life, and subjection to some degree of economic and social discrimination. This is precisely the complex that characterizes our high-delinquency areas. Such areas the incoming groups inhabit, groups generally of different ethnic or racial origin from that of the surrounding population, and the combination of resourcelessness and residential restrictions has resulted in increasingly congested and deteriorating housing, with multiple families occupying the space where a single family dwelt before.

It is the children of groups so situated that swell the delinquency statistics. For example, in New York City, in the first five months of 1959, 39 percent of the delinquency petitions before the Children's Court concerned Negro children, many of them from recently migrant Southern Negro families, and 22 percent concerned Puerto Rican children. The elementary and junior high-school enrollment in New York City public schools was given (October 31, 1958) as Negroes 21.3, and Puerto Ricans 16.3 percent. Various other evidences suggest that for the children of these two groups educational retardation is an important factor in the causation of delinquency.

The simple distinctions of delinquency incidence already drawn, which could be much more fully developed by a breakdown of delinquency statistics across the country, may be sufficient to refute some current misconceptions about the nature of the problem. In the first place, delinquency is not to be understood, as is sometimes done, as being essentially a "lower-class" phenomenon or as a product of "lower-class morality." Delinquency occurs among the youth of all classes, though in the more prosperous classes it may be less visible or less exposed and there is less among them of the petty filching that tempts the poor. Where delinquency is most prevalent, it is where particular evocative conditions exist, and these are to be found, not among the poor as a whole but especially among newly urbanized groups, ill-adjusted to city life and too frequently suffering the effects of social and economic prejudice and discrimination. We have therefore no ground to assume that the higher delinquency rates of these groups are attributable to inherent inferiority or native viciousness.

These considerations strengthen the prospect that the volume of juvenile delinquency can be definitely reduced by well-directed measures, based on an understanding of the conditions that foster it. If the higher rates are socially conditioned they should be amenable to constructive change in the conditions, including the timely provision of outlets, opportunities, and requisite training for the children who are beginning to seek illegitimate substitutes for them. But this is a topic to be developed later.

What the Statistics Really Mean

On the face of it, the growing delinquency statistics look quite alarming. In the decade 1948–1957 the number of juvenile delinquency court cases doubled for the country as a whole. The percent increase has been greatest in the last few years. If we project the 1957 rate it means that some 12 percent of all children between the ages of ten and seventeen will during their adolescence be involved in at least one court appearance on a delinquency charge. The number of youngsters who come to the attention of the police, without court appearance, is probably around three times as large. And when we note that boys are involved about five times as often as girls and also that considerably more urban boys are apprehended than rural boys, we reach the conclusion that any boy brought up in certain urban areas is almost as likely as not to run some time into some trouble with the law.

The delinquency problem is certainly a quite serious one, and clearly our attempts to deal with it have had little success. But again we shall misconceive both its dimensions and the nature of its demands on us unless we interpret aright these mounting figures.

Let us observe, to begin with, that the coverage of juvenile delinquency laws has become very wide, including a whole range of offenses from relatively trivial misbehavior to felonies. According to a somewhat old Children's Bureau report (1945)—more recent country-wide figures are not available—one-third of all charges, excluding traffic charges, before juvenile courts were on the ground of truancy or running away—forms of escapism that may not imply any evil intent. The proportion of very serious crimes, such as robbery or aggravated assault, was around only 2 percent. Moreover, the number of arrests depends somewhat on the activity of the police, and when the public is aroused by some flagrant juvenile crime the police are likely to apprehend a larger number than previously, which they can easily do because of the wide range of offenses that come within the scope of the delinquency laws. Potential arrests within the law are always greater than actual arrests, for adults and juveniles alike, and the disparity is lessened when there is public outcry. The other side of the picture is suggested in the fact that around half the cases brought before the courts are dismissed or discharged.

It may also be, as is frequently asserted, that greater public concern has been aroused in the needs and problems of our youth, and that in consequence more activity is displayed in reporting, recording, and handling cases of youthful misconduct. Youth welfare organizations, family organizations, clinics and institutions for delinquents have certainly increased, and a rather considerable proportion of the cases that come before our courts are referred by schools, psychiatric clinics, welfare organizations, and parents themselves. Another factor is a change that has come over the fights between youthful gangs. Scraps between teams or gangs of boys are probably as old as history, but in an age inured to violence the modern urban gang has taken to new and more deadly weapons. Instead of using fists and sticks and brickbats the embattled gang resorts to zip-guns and switch-blades and sawed-off shot guns, resulting in more serious and sometimes fatal casualties. When this happens, there is a public outcry for stronger measures of control, the police are alerted, and one way or another more youthful offenders come into evidence.

While, then, the vast increase in the reported rates of juvenile delinquency may not signify a *corresponding* increase in youthful misbehavior, it still reveals the gravity of the problem. Whatever affects youth affects the citizenship of tomorrow. The train of evils that follow from the disaffection, alienation, and lawlessness of youth is incalculably great—the squandering of energies, the degradation of families, the injury done to neighborhood and community, the mortgage on the society of the future, as well as the vast cost to the nation of crime itself. In some of our great cities the percentage of arrests for serious crimes has risen well over the earlier national average cited above.

What makes the problem more formidable is that in spite of the much-expanded agency activities directed to the control of delinquency the number of cases calling for such activities continues to increase. Is it then that these activities have little success, or should we assume that, had it not been for them, the increase would have been considerably greater? We might note in this connection that in 1956 and 1957 the number of juvenile court cases throughout the country rose more rapidly than in any preceding year.

Combating Delinquency

More light is needed on this whole subject. While some good studies have been made of certain institutions for delinquents and some exploration has been made of the efficacy of particular modes of treatment, the problem as a whole needs much fuller investigation. The public, while much concerned, is beset by a futile controversy between the advocates of strict disciplinary measures and the advocates of a social-service approach. Discipline is a necessary element of all upbringing, but mere discipline without effective appeal to mind and heart, so that it becomes one with self-discipline, is barren and causes revulsion. Discipline enforced by punishment alone neither improves the offender nor makes him less ready to offend again—but rather has a contrary effect. Those who believe sheer enforcement will stop delinquency—obviously it does not *reform* the delinquent—should learn something that criminology emphatically confirms, viz., that punishment, or more severe punishment, has never proved an effective deterrent of crime. Or they might consider, for example, the study of 500 delinquents made by the Gluecks, which found that 70 percent of the fathers were too strict or too erratic in the exercise of discipline, while 25 percent were lax or indifferent. It is time, then, we got beyond this unworthy controversy and faced the genuine issues.

In doing so, we should first distinguish between the two objectives of an overall program for the control of delinquency—prevention and rehabilitation. Much the major portion of the energy and expense devoted to the problem is concerned with rehabilitation. Too seldom do we find any well-thought-out project directed specifically to prevention. Yet practically all our authorities in this field agree that a preventive program—one planned to reach and re-orient young people at an earlier stage, when symptoms of incipient delinquency appear—has much the greater promise.

REHABILITATION. Let us look first at the rehabilitation problem. Here the agencies primarily involved are the police and the courts, though in a broader way we may regard the great majority of welfare agencies, both public and private, as having a significant part in it. The police on the one hand bring the large majority of cases before the courts, and on the other—since three-fourths of all youth dealt with by the police are not brought before the courts but simply ad-

monished, warned, sent back to their families, or referred
to some agency—have often the first opportunity to bring
influence to bear on erring youngsters. The degree to which
the police utilize this opportunity is very variant, depending on
the "philosophy" of the police department and the extent
to which they have a properly trained juvenile bureau or
division. It is wholly up to the courts to determine the degree
and kind of rehabilitative treatment for more serious cases.

Aside from such admonition and guidance as the particular
judge may offer in the brief process of the hearing and ad-
judication, the court has mainly the alternatives of probation
or institutionalization for cases that are not discharged or
dismissed. Around three times as many cases are put on
probation as are committed to institutions. Probation is certainly the more desirable alternative wherever there is no
clear necessity for institutional commitment, wherever, that
is, the youth can remain in his home environment without
serious peril to himself or to society.

While in principle the commitment of a juvenile to a cus-
todial institution, whether it be designated "training school,"
"residential treatment center," "youth camp," or otherwise,
is not punishment but a remedial or rehabilitative measure,
it none the less deprives him of liberty and relegates him for
a period ranging generally from around eight months up to
two or more years to a restrictive unnatural environment. He
is cut off from home and associates and neighborhood. His
effective society consists of a group of similarly resentful delinquent youth, under the control of a body of officials and
professional workers. No matter how devoted and how skilled

this latter body may be, they are often unable to make head-
way against the "underworld" spirit that develops in the
rebellious youth. The relatively innocent ones among them
may learn more evil ways from the tougher ones, and the latter
are likely to bully the former and subject them to indignities
and even to the pent-up sexual desires that are roused under
such conditions. The recidivism rate is generally quite high.

These are adequate grounds for preferring the alternative
of probation wherever it is admissible. Since, however, some
cases do call for institutional custody and care, every precau-
tion should be taken to limit the risks of this process. Experience shows that small-scale institutions are preferable to
large-scale ones. Small-scale institutions admit of more spe-
cialization, closer personal relations, and more experimenta-
tion. The broad term "delinquency" covers many different
kinds of behavior trouble, requiring differential treatment.
And when delinquent tendencies are associated with particular physical or mental ailments, specialized institutions to
deal with different types of problem are clearly indicated.
Wherever feasible, small urban residential shelters and group
foster homes should be developed, and most of all for such
delinquent boys or girls as may be institutionalized because
their proper homes are deemed unfit for them to live in.

Whatever may be achieved in the above-mentioned respects, the alternative of probation offers the greater promise,
for all except the very serious or difficult cases. But it has to
be effective probation. Too often probation is a wholly
perfunctory service. Too often it is understood to mean
merely a routine check every few months to find whether

the youngster has been in trouble again. Caseloads are often
far too heavy, and even where reasonable qualifications are
set up for probation officers the screening is too often ineffec-
tive and the salaries are too low to attract an adequately
equipped staff. There are some outstanding exceptions, where
the nature and the requirements of a probation system for
juvenile offenders are properly realized. But the country as a
whole is very far from having attained this level.

Since probation is the primary service provided under the
courts for the rehabilitation of erring youngsters, it must be
developed to serve as far as possible this objective. The probation officer should have the qualification, the time, and the
opportunity to offer help, protection, and guidance. He
should have the ability to recognize the different types of
trouble that affect young delinquents and to enlist the appropriate services of voluntary agencies and official ones alike.
He should familiarize himself with the family background
and the youth's case history. He should either be in frequent
contact himself with the youth or else find some "big
brother," settlement worker, or good neighbor who will do
so. The requisite service places a high responsibility on the
probation officer and involves the additional cost of a considerably larger probation staff than is usual. But the extra
cost per youth is quite small compared with the cost of institutionalization and weighs a trifle in the balance against
the benefit of rehabilitation.

PREVENTION. From rehabilitative measures we turn to preventive ones. As already pointed out, the potentialities of
well-thought-out preventive services still lie largely in the

future, though in recent years some definite advances have been made. We have more knowledge of the conditions under which delinquency develops, of the early indications of delinquent tendencies, and of the different types of behavior disorder that we lump together under the term "delinquency." This growing knowledge is beginning—though only beginning—to result in more promising action-programs. We are beginning to realize the high importance of early screening so as to discover the tensions and problems of children, as a pre-condition of providing guidance and needed care. Here is a function the schools are peculiarly well situated to fulfill, and in various school areas throughout the country programs are being inaugurated or developed for this purpose. We are learning that the mere provision of more playgrounds and better recreational facilities and occasional summer camps, valuable as these are in themselves, does not reach the heart of the deeper-seated conflicts and troubles that beset the disoriented children of our congested slums and semi-ghettos. And maybe we are also beginning to perceive that the social work approach, however valuable for the rescue and redirection of juveniles who are getting into trouble, does not suffice to change the environmental conditions and the socio-economic factors that breed the habits of delinquency.

The prevention of delinquency may be thought of in two ways. In the broader sense, whatever can be achieved in the upbringing and education of children, whatever influences can be brought to bear to arouse constructive interests in them, whatever parents first, then school and church and associations, can do to understand the problems and the needs of youth, to evoke their capacities and to sustain their morale —all such up-building influences are preventives of serious delinquency. But these generalities have no bite. Possibly, if we take them from the reverse side they may have more practical relevance. Thus, delinquency is prevented by whatever can be done to guide parents to avoid either laxness or too rigid discipline with their children, by whatever can be done to enable young persons to find their own interests and discover their capacities, by whatever the school system can do to insure more stimulating and personalized teaching, particularly for pupils who are irked by schooling or who are slow to learn.

In a more specific sense the prevention of delinquency may be regarded as the rescue of those young persons who are showing symptoms of delinquent tendencies or forming habits or making associations that may well lead to a delinquent career. It is necessary, however, to distinguish between mere prankishness, mischief-making, and boyish aggressiveness on the one hand and the more ominous indications of disaffection, alienation, and antisocial attitudes on the other. We proceed to cite three types of specific preventive programs classified according to the breadth of their operation.

1. The first type centers directly on the affected young people, on the individual boys and girls who exhibit the earlier signs of behavior trouble which, unless arrested, may develop into confirmed habits of delinquency. Such "pre-delinquents" may be reached through school contacts, agency referrals, or neighborhood investigation. It is a first-aid service,

endeavoring initially to enlist their interest, cooperation, and friendship, offering them help in their troubles and problems, seeking to redirect their attitudes, endeavoring in the process to understand their situation, to deal with such sources of conflict as may lie in their family relationships, school relationships, or peer-age associations, and seeking to provide for them outlets and opportunities they lack. It is a task that requires much patience and skill. For some cases special professional service, medical, psychiatric, or other, may need to be called in.

While such programs can and do render quite valuable service—and the earlier they get to the disturbed child, the more successful they are likely to be—there remains always the serious danger that the continued impact of an unfavorable environment may undo this temporary effect.

2. The second type of program seeks to minimize this danger. It concentrates on the neighborhood itself and endeavors to provide for young people within it some of the sustainment that otherwise is lacking. Under this type we include, for example, the Chicago Area Project, which is distinctive in that its primary concern is to set up areal organizations composed of residents of high-delinquency areas, so as to enlist them in active concern for the welfare of neighborhood youth. Such organizations are not likely to arise spontaneously in these areas, and in any case they need outside resources. The Project, while scrupulous to leave decisions in the hands of the residents themselves, has been successful in mobilizing such organizations and in aiding them to carry out a variety of programs for youth recreation and for

the training of delinquent juveniles, as well as campaigns for
measures of community improvement. The Area Project
recognizes that neighborhood organizations of this kind offer
by no means the whole answer to the delinquency problem,
but regards the alerted participation of neighborhood residents as an essential aspect of it.

Another kind of neighborhood planning, which in the first
instance is not specifically directed to the delinquency situation but has important implications for it, is that of the All-
Day Neighborhood Schools of New York City. There are
now nine of these schools situated in the neediest and most
run-down areas of the city. While regular elementary schools
under the Board of Education, they utilize special services
extending beyond school hours and are occupied with community activities in the evening. The core of the operation
is a team of six "group teachers," with an administrator.
These teachers work from 11 to 5, carrying on flexible educational programs through the school hours and from 3 to 5
conducting various recreational programs through "clubs,"
one for each grade. The "clubs" are composed of children
whose parents work late and others who may particularly
need this opportunity. During the recreation period the psychiatric social worker unobtrusively observes and gives aid to
children in need of special attention. Other services are
provided through volunteers, and the school receives additional equipment and resources through the local branch of
the Citizens for the All-Day Neighborhood Schools, an organization that has done much to support the system. (Special programs are also carried on during the summer.) Every

effort is being made during school hours and beyond them to provide some cultural enrichment for these deprived children.

The schools are open evenings for meetings and discussions of neighborhood issues. The ADNS plan seeks to enlist the interest of the adults both in the work of the schools and in the civic and social needs of the neighborhood. It is hard sledding under the circumstances, but some progress is achieved. In addition to the group teacher staff each school has an ADNS administrator; three have also a special "community coordinator," and the whole system is in charge of a devoted director who has under the Board of Education been the principal founder and formulator of the ADNS plan.

Even a casual visitor to an ADNS school can hardly fail to be impressed by the spirit animating it, by the happy responsiveness of pupils, and the friendly relations between teacher and taught. They are not all equally successful in these respects—it takes some time for the plan to catch hold in new schools—but the prevailing attitude contradicts the old conception of the balky child, "creeping like a snail unwillingly to school." Truancy is conspicuously less frequent than is characteristic of schools situated in slum-like areas, and since chronic truancy goes hand in hand with delinquency we can reasonably infer that the ADNS schools have preventive efficacy. A study is now being planned to test this inference.

As a third example of a neighborhood-oriented program it may be in order to mention one recently inaugurated in New York City under the sponsorship of the President of

the New York City Council and of the Juvenile Delinquency
Evaluation Project. The Project in question, set up by the
mayor in 1956, is the first investigation so far undertaken
of the whole operation of a great city in the field of juvenile
delinquency. It studies and reports on the functions, the
problems, the needs, and the interrelations of all the official
agencies involved, and also considers the role played by a
considerable variety of voluntary agencies. In addition the
Project has now undertaken, with the support of the city's
Youth Board, to organize an experimental program for the
prevention of delinquency in one high-delinquency neighborhood in the Bronx.

In briefest outline the program is directed to reach the
near-delinquents or pre-delinquents, establishing a system of
continuous contacts with the people and the agencies of the
neighborhood, to bring them "first aid" through the minis-
trations of its own staff, to guide them to needed agency
services, to inquire into their family relations, school relations, and other possible sources of trouble, to provide recreational and other outlets and assist them in matters of training and potential employment, and to keep a thorough record of case histories, of services rendered, and of services
called for but not adequately available. At the same time the
program is promoting a neighborhood council for the well-
being of neighborhood children and a body of local volunteers to assist the professional staff in the discovery of neighborhood needs.

3. Finally, we turn to the third and most far-reaching type
of preventive program. Our second type went beyond the first

by envisaging the neighborhood as a whole—endeavoring to mobilize it for the service of its youth in trouble. Our third type, taken in its totality, is perhaps nowhere fully realized, though some approaches to it exist, and others are now being planned. It would thoroughly renovate the physical neighborhood itself, removing the conditions that stimulate and confirm habits, attitudes, ways of living that in themselves are prejudicial to decent citizenship—the congestion, the litter, the promiscuity, the decaying multi-partitioned housing, the cramped ugly yards, the whole physical impoverishment that in certain city areas is the accompaniment and the accomplice of economic and social impoverishment.

We have here in view not the sporadic delinquency that occurs in every area, among every class of the population, but the more concentrated and formidable volume of delinquency that characterizes the deteriorated areas of our great cities. These high-delinquency areas are typically areas to which incoming groups, usually of a different ethnic or racial stock from the surrounding population, entering the great city from an agricultural background and at the lowest economical level, have accommodated themselves. A whole complex of conditions work against their proper integration into the fabric of American society and turn the areas they inhabit into festering slums that have a deleterious effect on the welfare of the city as a whole. Every adverse factor helps to perpetuate every other—the physical setting, the impoverishment in a land of plenty, the abrupt change from old ways of living, the cultural denudation as the traditional culture loses hold on the young and the new one is slow to be acquired, the lack of training and of adequate opportunities and outlets for youthful energies, and the social and economic discrimination that so frequently is aroused by the rest of the complex. Perhaps one should rather be surprised that so large a proportion of those subjected to these conditions are able to surmount them than that a sizable minority of the young go seriously astray.

While some steps are being taken to improve certain of these conditions, no more than very partial success can be looked for so long as the delinquency-breeding physical slum continues to exist as the habitation of these new urban groups. Great housing schemes under public auspices are certainly of high merit, especially if those who go to live within them are given accessory social services. But they merely bound the areas of deterioration and are in danger of being infected by them. A thorough program of renovation, reconstruction, maintenance, inspection, limitation of subdividing, and overall control is a major need, with adequate provision for recreation, youth clubs, and other neighborhood amenities. With this physical basis other programs for neighborhood upbuilding, such as those already described, would have much better prospects. As for the cost of these measures, it would be repaid abundantly in the ultimate economic saving, and many times over in the social and moral gain to the city as a whole, and most of all to its troubled youth.

To organize all-out neighborhood programs for the areas of in-migration it would be advantageous for such large cities as are involved to set up special commissions, one for each incoming group. Such a commission would investigate the needs and problems of the group and the conditions of any neighborhood in which it settles. It would include housing experts, educators, and representatives of relevant city agencies and of welfare organizations. An all-out enterprise of this sort would, for the first time in our history, assure that these incoming groups would start afresh, protected against the demoralizing conditions to which in the past they have so often been subjected, and thus enabled to develop their proper contribution to our multi-group society.

We observe in conclusion that programs for the prevention of juvenile delinquency have the great advantage over programs of rehabilitation in that they benefit whole groups, while reaching to those who are in special danger. And the more thorough the program of prevention the more far-spreading is the service it renders. A full-scale neighborhood program is of benefit to the whole community. While it saves some from becoming delinquents it contributes no less to the well-being of the many who are resistant to that danger, and to their elders as well. Wherever we find a high rate of delinquency we can be sure that the root trouble lies not in the youth themselves, but in the social and environmental conditions to which they and their families have been exposed.

FRONTIERS IN VOLUNTARY WELFARE SERVICES

by ELIZABETH WICKENDEN

ALMOST all Americans know something about voluntary social welfare services for children and young people. The annual Community Chest campaign with its familiar red feather symbol; the Boy Scouts, Girl Scouts, and Camp Fire Girls; the American Red Cross; the YM and YWCA; the youth-serving and children's programs of their own religious denominations; the Salvation Army; the family service, child welfare, and settlement house agencies in their own communities; the Travelers Aid beacon when they travel: these and many others are familiar aspects of the American social environment. But not everyone, even when actively involved in these programs, has paused to consider just how any particular method of making provision for the needs of children and young people differs from the many other organizational devices used to meet similar needs and how it is related to the evolution of the social structure as a whole. A broad appraisal of the way in which American social insti-

Elizabeth Wickenden is Consultant on Public Social Policy to the National Social Welfare Assembly.

tutions are serving or failing our younger generation in this pivotal year of 1960 must necessarily take into account the evolving pattern of social welfare services under voluntary auspices.

There are three aspects of this question. First, we are here concerned with a specific *function*, known as "social welfare," with characteristics that distinguish it from other youth-serving functions such as education, health, and recreation. Second, we are discussing these services under *auspices* described as "voluntary" to distinguish them from those provided by governmental bodies under the compulsion of law. What relationships and distinctions exist between these two auspices and how have they developed? Third, our appraisal focuses upon welfare services in a particular *setting*—the United States at this period in its history. No function is more directly the product and the instrument of the society it serves and hence more dependent upon the immediate setting within which it operates. But understanding this present, with its implications for the future, requires in turn historical perspective.

The Functional Evolution

Two functions are basic to any society: protection of children through their dependency period and their induction into the culture of the society in which they live. In all human societies these functions are shared with the individual mother by a widening circle of other individuals cooperating for these purposes under a variety of institutional patterns. First to join the mother in this responsibility is

the father, and their continued association in the task of
child nurture creates the fundamental social institution, the
family. Around the nuclear family there develop broadening
circles of responsibility, initially bound by ties of consan-
guinity and marriage, and subsequently by propinquity, a
common base of economic operation, and a shared culture.

In a society which is relatively localized, stable, and simple
in its functioning, the family, village, or tribal pattern of relationship adequately meets the socially recognized needs of
children in virtually all circumstances. More organized social
measures for this specific purpose are not only not available
but, under prevailing social standards, they are neither needed
nor missed. In such a society the larger family circle simply
closes around and absorbs the child who suffers any failure
in parental care. Similarly in this kind of social setting cultural assimilation of the up-coming generation proceeds along
traditionally prescribed lines until outside influence or basic
changes of social organization disturb the pattern.

BEGINNINGS OF SOCIAL WELFARE. Organized welfare services
appear on the social scene when something happens to upset the elementary equilibrium between individual, family,
and society. This most commonly results from basic changes
in the methods and organization of economic production
affecting in turn all other social relationships. Or, it might
result from large-scale migration disrupting the family and
cultural pattern, or from war or conquest. Outside influence
might be brought to bear through trading or colonization
or evangelization—or, in our more popular modern terms,
technical assistance and the communication of ideas. Any

such disturbance of the status quo can set off a chain reaction of social readjustment wherein the former pattern no longer meets the needs of children.

At the same time any change in social organization and social aspiration inevitably affects the objectives and methods of child-rearing. This is clear in our own era with its steadily increasing complexity of social organization. The task of rearing children to independent adult functioning takes longer, involves the application of more specialized knowledge, and becomes constantly more costly and progressively more complex. Individual parents are less able to fulfill their obligation to or their aspirations for their children without the aid of organized social support. The almost universal development of schools to share the parental task of cultural preparation is a clear example of this. Social welfare services are likewise a way to supplement and support the family in assuring to children the help they need in growing up into a complex, hazardous, and challenging social environment.

Social welfare is simply the organized measures through which society provides assurance that the recognized social needs of individuals will be met and that those social relationships and adjustments considered necessary to its own functioning will be facilitated. Social welfare services for children are, therefore, correspondingly those which supplement, support, or, when necessary, substitute for the family in providing the standard of protective care and nurture a particular social group deems necessary for its dependent members; and those considered necessary to facilitate the social assimilation of young people as functioning members of that particular society or social group. The term "social standard" describes this interaction of social entitlement and social obligation underlying the welfare function.

No definition comfortably fits the facts of social welfare experience unless it recognizes the variability of this standard in different settings, stages of historical evolution, and among individual groups in a pluralistic society. These variations in social standard provide the central dynamic in the evolution of the social welfare function.

EARLY INSTITUTIONS. Organized child welfare service seems typically to begin as congregate care in institutions. Misleadingly called "orphanages," these institutions have generally made provision not for children who had lost their parents but for children who would benefit by being segregated from the prevailing low level of care available in their homes. Beginning in the Middle Ages children's institutions, usually under religious sponsorship, not only provided care for the orphans created by the wars, pestilence, and social change of the period, but also pioneered in the new educational and health services demanded by a changing social order. The Elizabethan Poor Laws also made institutional provision for children under governmental auspices through the almshouse. Both types were brought to this country by its settlers to serve as forerunners of present voluntary and public child welfare programs. The general-purpose children's institution seen today in less-developed countries outlived its historical purpose in our own country when changing social standards demanded more specialized services and decried the isolation of children from the mainstream of family and community life.

DEVELOPMENT OF DIFFERENTIATED CHILD WELFARE SERVICES. Toward the end of the nineteenth century social services for children began to develop rapidly in terms of scope and differentiation, and thus required more complex organization and specialized staffing. Out of these and related needs the structure of modern social welfare and the profession of social work were born. The change in children's services can be attributed to three factors: changes of attitude regarding children's developmental needs, changes in social needs and organization resulting from industrialization, and—for the United States—the peculiar task of assimilating millions of newcomers into our social structure. Each of these factors helped to shape American social services in this generative period.

Social and psychological sciences emphasized the essential role of individual family nurture in child development, especially in the early years. Consequently a variety of services directed toward assuring an adequately functioning family base for every child gradually displaced the earlier reliance on institutional care. Special children's agencies were organized to bring together parentless children and childless couples through adoption and to find temporary foster family care for those requiring it. By the same logic every effort was made to hold together families threatened by psychological tensions or economic deprivation. Charitable organizations (predecessors of today's family service agencies) provided counseling services, economic aid, and other services to such families.

Other services developed that were directed toward supplementing family care in order to meet special needs requiring the more specialized services opened up by advancing science. Social welfare often plays a pioneering role in this respect by initiating services which later become programs with a broader base of social responsibility. Many specialized educational, health, recreation, and related programs began in this way as charitable undertakings of particular religious or other voluntary groups. This aspect of the welfare function derives from the fact that particular groups are committed to a standard of social obligation toward children not yet accepted by the whole society. Through voluntary association they pioneer in new areas which in turn raise the sights and ultimately the standards of others.

A third type of welfare service is related to the problem of acculturation and particularly to the processes by which young people are prepared for the social responsibilities of adult life. This became a major task when millions of immigrants were coming to this country, and early American social work took much of its own coloration from historical circumstance. Child-rearing became an especially complex task when children were growing up in a culture new to their parents. Such parents found it difficult to assist their children and parent-child conflicts were aggravated by these differences. Socially organized measures were, therefore, increasingly necessary and rapidly expanded under the auspices of religious bodies, settlement houses, and other voluntary organizations. At the same time the shift from a frontier-type agricultural economy to one characterized by large-scale industrial production and urban living created tensions and problems of adjustment for young people that still persist.

Social welfare also sought to help children in a fourth and broadly pervasive way: by striving for an adjustment of prevailing social values and existing social institutions in order better to meet their needs. This crusading aspect of the welfare function played a major role in its formative years. Efforts to achieve protective legislation, limitations on child labor, better public welfare programs, improved juvenile courts, changing attitudes and opportunities for the children of minority groups, and the successive White House Conferences on the needs of children launched in 1909 are all examples of this area of welfare activity.

Voluntary and Government Auspices

Social welfare services perform the same social functions under either voluntary or governmental auspices. No absolute distinctions can be made, especially in our social system that encourages pluralistic approaches to the same problem. Whether the adoption of a particular child is arranged by the welfare agency of his parents' faith, by a nonsectarian voluntary agency, or by the local public welfare department, its social purpose is the same: to provide him with a home. There are, however, certain attributes in each which tend toward a differentiation in functional emphasis.

In general voluntary services reflect the active concern of particular groups within a society, while those under government auspices are largely directed toward needs so widespread or so compelling that the authority of law and the taxing power are brought to bear on meeting them. Thus voluntary services tend toward variability and those under government toward universality. But services which are initially varied may move toward universality as the need or desire for them becomes more widely recognized. Historically this has produced a steady movement from voluntary toward governmental sponsorship for widely accepted welfare services, a movement fostered by the voluntary agencies themselves as the scope of particular needs became apparent in their own selective undertakings.

Voluntary welfare has, however, continued to carry forward its own adaptive function by pioneering in the development of new services, continuing as pacemaker in some fields entered by government, and focusing on functions for which they feel a special competence or responsibility. Religious agencies, especially those of minority faiths, feel a compelling obligation to provide services for the children and young people of their own group in order to protect their religious and cultural heritage. The American tradition of reliance on mutual aid has also helped to sustain the vitality of voluntary welfare and leads to continuous invention, of which recent examples might be seen in such peripheral developments as the union health and welfare fund, Alcoholics Anonymous, and the cooperative nursery school.

There are also countervailing factors tending to becloud these characteristic distinctions. As public welfare has become universally established and widely accepted, it has developed a wide variety of new services which not only parallel those of voluntary agencies but may, in particular communities, outstrip them. At the same time private agencies have been increasingly financed by tax money in the performance of functions the government considers essential. This confusion in traditional social role has not yet been assimilated in social welfare theory, much of which derives from the time when voluntary agency pioneering was creating a new social function and a new profession.

INFLUENCES ON VOLUNTARY WELFARE. Modern social welfare services were largely initiated under voluntary auspices. Though minimal governmental protection against dependency had existed since Poor Law days, the scientific and professionally oriented approach of the new agencies was more a protest against this undifferentiated and humiliating public program than its progeny. The impulse and drive for the new services came from many sources. Religious conviction then and now played an important role and religious bodies lent their institutional support, both as sponsors of services for their own members and backers of community effort. The volunteer, contributing his effort as well as his money, is intrinsic to any successful voluntary welfare undertaking. The established agency of today was once created from nothing by dedicated people whose breadth of vision was their only professional qualification for the new field of social welfare. The philanthropic impulse which led successful community leaders to discharge their sense of social responsibility toward newcomers and other disadvantaged neighbors in financial support for these new agencies was indispensable to their growth. In time this burgeoning social welfare field also developed a source of strength and support in the profession of social work, itself largely fostered by the early voluntary agencies.

THE INFLUENCE OF PUBLIC WELFARE DEVELOPMENT. Voluntary social welfare led the way, but, under the pressures of economic and social change, governmental welfare development was not far behind. From the turn of the century governmental programs expanded rapidly, and they were vastly accelerated by the depression. This growth, encouraged by voluntary agencies that saw clearly the need for broader-based measures than they could provide, has inevitably had a profound impact in turn on the functioning of the voluntary agencies, an impact that can be considered in three ways.

In the first place large-scale public programs, especially those that prevent or relieve economic need, have greatly modified the character of voluntary programs. The various Social Security measures, launched in 1935 following earlier emergency relief provisions, have virtually eliminated the need for voluntary agencies to give economic aid to the needy except in unusual circumstances. By providing for needy children and the survivors of insured workers, these programs have also virtually eliminated dependency as a cause of child placement. Governmental programs in the fields of health, education, housing, vocational placement, race relations, and many others have likewise affected the character of voluntary welfare activity for children and their parents.

Governmental financing of voluntary agencies to perform welfare services in its behalf is a second important influence. This may take several forms. Most common is the purchase of a specified service from a voluntary agency by the public welfare agency or children's court in behalf of a particular child or family for which it has assumed responsibility. Less widespread is the outright governmental subsidy paid to a voluntary agency to underwrite its performance of a needed welfare function, for example, day care for the children of working mothers, or services directed toward potential delinquents. Another device, more widely used in the health field, involves grants to voluntary agencies for research and demonstration projects in a particular problem field. And finally the federal government gives substantial financial aid to nonprofit agencies by authorizing the deduction from taxable income of individual, corporate, or foundation contributions to organizations engaged in recognized charitable, educational, and related activity. Similar concessions are made by state and local governments in exemptions from property, excise, sales and other taxes.

Governmental influence is also applied directly through regulation and the power to enforce suspension of activity. This usually takes the form of licensing, which requires that individuals or agencies performing certain services meet specified minimum standards. Child-caring agencies are commonly licensed and generally welcome this limited public regulation in order to protect the standards of child welfare practice from unscrupulous or poorly qualified individuals and organizations. The solicitation of funds for charitable purposes is also subject to regulation in many states in order to prevent fraud.

THE INFLUENCE OF FEDERATION. Another major influence on voluntary welfare development has been the rapid growth in the last forty years of federated fund-raising at the community level as a means of channeling philanthropic giving through one annual campaign and one allocating mechanism. At present 2,027 American communities with approximately 115 million residents are served by community chests, united funds, and similar organizations. Approximately $400,000,000 was raised during 1959 to provide funds for 27,000 separate voluntary agencies.

Federation plays such a dominant role in shaping the prevailing voluntary welfare philosophy that its impact is difficult to appraise. On the one hand it has served to reduce public irritation arising from a multiplicity of fund appeals, has encouraged efficient use of community and professional energies in a single concentrated campaign, and has subjected the operation of all participating agencies to periodic review by an objective citizen group—thus protecting the public and encouraging the agencies to adapt to changing needs and concepts. A logical corollary has been the development of community welfare councils, now functioning in 438 communities, to plan and coordinate welfare and related community services. On the negative side there has recently developed some revolt against federated fund-raising on the ground that it dilutes the principal asset of voluntarism, its capacity for giving practical expression to the aspirations,

particular interests, and special needs of different groups
in the population.

THE INFLUENCE OF CORPORATE GIVING AND THE LABOR MOVE-
MENT. Two other influences of growing importance in voluntary welfare are those of the corporate giver, as represented
by industry and foundations, and the labor movement. Forty
percent of the money raised by community funds comes
from business and 40 percent from workers, the latter actively
encouraged by their unions. The former represents an important source of contribution which, because it is passed
on to the consumer and tax-payer, seems relatively painless.
Again, however, it tends toward dilution of one of the traditional values of voluntarism: the close rapport between
giver, service, and beneficiary. This is offset to some extent
by the growing labor representation in voluntary welfare
management and financing, since the unions tend to think
of themselves as representing both the giver and the beneficiary. In both cases, however, an additional organizational
structure is added to the voluntary equation.

The Current Social Setting

In our time, as in all others, the particular characteristics of
social welfare services for children and youth depend upon:
1) the special problems of adaptation confronting our society; 2) the social standard it applies to the rights, obligation, and role of its children and their families; 3) its economic capacity to provide the benefits and services required
by the first two; and 4) the extent to which children's needs
are met by nonwelfare measures. The interaction of these

factors is sharply revealed when efforts are made to export
the standards and supporting institutions of one society to
another with differing adaptive problems. For example, the
social standard represented by child labor laws is quite impractical in a country where the very survival of children
depends on their productivity and where there is no educational system to occupy the years thus added to their developmental period.

In our own setting the startling growth of productive capacity (now approaching a money value of $500 billion
a year) has made possible a national income which not only
does not depend upon the employment of children but provides a substantial surplus which can be applied to their
extended rearing. Thus a primary characteristic of our society
is the prolongation of the period of youthful dependency
and the greatly increased social investment, both through
family expenditure and socially provided services, in the up-
coming generation. The growing proportion of this investment financed by government in the form of public schools,
public health, public recreation, public welfare, and other
public services has affected both family budgeting and voluntary services.

THE PRESENT CHALLENGE. At the same time the rapid change
in institutional structure, population distribution, social attitudes and values that has been necessary to produce this
rising standard have, in their turn, produced new problems of
social adaptation, especially for the young. These tensions
and maladjustments today constitute the principal challenge
to voluntary social welfare. The time when poverty and eco-

nomic insecurity spawned the major social problems is gradually giving way to one characterized chiefly by changes in social relationships and values. While pockets of economic injustice remain, the disequilibrium between individuals and their social environment that more particularly characterizes our time is revealed in such widespread symptomatic social problems as divorce, family desertion, illegitimacy, juvenile delinquency, alcoholism, drug addiction, mental illness or personality disturbance, and the phenomenon called by social scientists *anomie* or alienation between individuals and the society in which they live.

These problems offer a particular challenge to voluntary agencies. This is true whether they are regarded as transitional problems arising from the struggle of contemporary man to move to a higher level of social functioning or, as some maintain, to a decline in basic morality and standards of social responsibility. In either case—and they are not mutually exclusive—the adaptive capacity of our pluralistic democratic system is directly challenged. It is twice challenged, since it is also being subjected to critical testing by the growth abroad of a competing system characterized by unitary authority rooted in a concept of predetermined historic dynamic. The conflict between democracy and Communism is more likely to be resolved by the relative effectiveness of the two systems in resolving these social problems of our day than by a clash of arms that would destroy both.

Children are the inevitable victims of social disequilibrium, for their emotional and social development depends upon the emotional and social health of the individuals and institutions surrounding them. Emotionally disturbed or immature parents leave the emotional needs of children unsatisfied. Broken families deprive them of the social matrix on which their best development depends. Prolonged economic dependency of young people intensifies normal tensions between generations and extends the gap between biological maturity and the time when marriage is economically feasible. Rapidly shifting social patterns and values complicate the already difficult transition from childhood to adulthood represented by adolescence. Tensions created by past wars, the cold war, and the threat of future war—including the interruption of normal living caused by compulsory military service—encourage withdrawal from social responsibility on the part of some young people whether in the guise of indifferent conformity to the status quo, the active rebellion of juvenile delinquency, or the passive anarchy of so-called "beat generation" disaffiliation. Growing up in our time presents all of these hazards for young people. Even though many find within themselves and their immediate social environment the sources of their own growth—as previous generations have done before them—voluntary welfare agencies find the emphasis of their traditional adaptive role shifting to these developmental problems and pressures, seeking to ease their impact on individuals and advance compensatory institutional change.

The central role of the family in child nurture remains undiminished by the changes in its composition and functioning that have accompanied changes in the total institutional pattern. In fact, the strength and stability represented for the child by his own family becomes proportionately more crucial as the larger society imposes the heavier demands implicit in rapid change and increasing complexity. At the same time the family is subjected by these same factors to pressures that constitute a direct challenge to social welfare. The shrinkage in family size and its isolation from binding identity with a larger social group have placed an unprecedented burden on the nuclear family and especially on the parent-child relationship. Frequent movement from one locality to another tends to intensify this isolation. Early marriage, seemingly a product of youthful insecurity, the widespread employment of mothers outside the home, the changing social pattern in masculine-feminine roles, and the uncertain application of psychological theory to family relationships have all contributed to the current insecurities in family life. To the extent that these insecurities derive from social causes, the remedy likewise must be found in social measures.

Voluntary welfare agencies seek to strengthen the family, both in its normal functioning and in times of crisis, by three types of help. Family agencies help relieve internal tensions by bringing objective counsel to bear on emotional and other family problems and by helping secure more specialized assistance, such as psychiatric or other forms of therapeutic service, when needed. Welfare agencies of many types also help relieve the family by providing supplementary services for its children. Visiting housekeeper service that helps keep families together when the mother is ill or absent from the home clearly demonstrates the institutionalization of a service formerly assured by the larger family or neighborhood. With almost one-third of the mothers of children under eighteen working, day care centers meet a pressing realistic need and, many social workers believe, contribute to family stability by easing social and emotional pressures that many mothers cannot otherwise withstand. Recreational and other group activity for young people outside the home, including summer camping, are also characteristic ways to strengthen the family by supplementing its benefits and relieving its internal pressures. Parent education and discussion groups offer the traditional reassurance of shared experience, reinforced by objective counsel. Controversies surrounding the institutionalization of many social functions formerly centered in the home seem to miss the reciprocal value of this trend in freeing the basic emotional vitality of the family relationship.

Welfare agencies also continue to find, when and if family care fails, substitutes in the form of adoptive or foster home placement. Increasingly, however, these children are the victims of social maladjustment rather than economic conditions or death in the family. Illegitimacy, family breakdown, or emotional difficulties account for an increasing proportion of these children. The close relationship between child placement and family service is thus emphasized and many combined agencies have resulted. Religious agencies are especially, though not exclusively, concerned with the provision of these substitutes for family care, partly because of charitable tradition and partly because of the principle, incorporated in many state laws, that children should be assured religious rearing in their own faith. Couples seeking children for adoption continue to outnumber the available supply except where children of certain minority groups and those with special handicaps are involved. This fact—together with upheavals abroad and widespread travel by Americans in military or foreign service—has resulted in the increasing adoption of foreign children with concomitant legal and social problems for welfare agencies to resolve.

In providing services for children with special needs, the welfare function changes conspicuously as new needs develop and as well-established services are taken over by others. Thus services for blind and deaf children—to cite one example—initiated under welfare auspices are increasingly incorporated into the educational system. At the same time welfare agencies carry forward their traditional pioneering function by spurring the development of experimental or intensive service in such fields as the treatment of children with severe emotional disturbance, the mentally retarded, and rehabilitation of the physically handicapped. As the need for general-purpose orphanages has diminished, institutional care for children has centered on those requiring highly specialized treatment and those whose own developmental needs are better served by group living arrangements.

Voluntary welfare agencies are also concerned with children whose special needs derive from minority or newcomer status as with the Negroes and Puerto Ricans in many cities, from the migratory nature of the family occupation, from the military service of the father, or from the fact that they are away from home or traveling. Another important area of voluntary welfare service involves aid to needy children overseas. This includes both direct aid in the form of food, clothing, and medical supplies, and technical assistance to help countries develop their own child welfare programs. Many have also sponsored international student exchange, work-camp, and study-tour programs for young people as their contribution to helping prepare for life in a shrinking world.

The transition from childhood dependency to adult self-reliance and social responsibility is not easy in any age or culture. In our own time it seems especially difficult for many young people for such reasons as changing social values, increasing organizational complexity, world tension, excessive pressure on the family, prolonged dependency, and heavy social demands in such forms as military service, technical knowledge, widening scope of social identification, and unceasing adaptability.

Voluntary agencies help bridge the gap by sponsoring programs that combine group association on a peer basis with mature leadership. These programs are often under religious sponsorship—such as the YM and YWCA, the YM and YWHA, Catholic Youth Organization and Jewish Center programs—both as a means of preserving cultural and religious traditions and as a logical link between home and the larger society. The neighborhood is also a natural center and many housing projects make provisions to house a voluntary welfare agency for this purpose. This is a peculiarly institutional function, since the family cannot effectively wean its adolescents itself and self-organization by adolescents may isolate them from the very society they are seeking to join.

Juvenile delinquency represents one measure of the failure

of this process and today constitutes a major, and in some cities critical, challenge to the welfare function. Voluntary welfare services are directed both to the prevention of overt antisocial activity by rebellious young people and to the salvaging of those already involved, including those coming before the juvenile courts. An interesting example of preventive work involves the assignment of social workers by neighborhood houses and other agencies to work with youthful street gangs in an effort to channel their mutual loyalty and cohesiveness into constructive outlets. Agencies have also assigned caseworkers to seek out on a so-called "aggressive" basis the families of potential delinquents in an effort to strengthen the family base and hence the child's development. Many voluntary agencies also operate institutional and other programs for delinquent children who are either committed to them by the courts or sent by their parents or guardians on a voluntary basis. Here again religious motivation often plays an important role, but programs under both denominational and secular auspices have increasingly added psychiatric concepts of treatment to the traditional vocational training of such schools. Post-institutional aid and supervision is also provided by many voluntary agencies.

The social problems of children today can never be solved through the provision of more and better welfare services. In fact one of the frequent criticisms directed at social welfare is that it attempts to bale out the ocean of social maladjustment with the teacup of individual services. This criticism is justifiable only to the extent that welfare agencies, especially the voluntary agencies with their greater freedom in this respect, fail to use their knowledge of individual problems to remedy the social conditions that cause them or to improve the social institutions that might prevent them. There are three ways voluntary agencies can do this. Through research, both especially organized projects and analysis of their regular programs, they can establish the facts regarding children's present problems and the efficacy of existing measures. Through planning devices—community welfare councils, conferences, and the many committees that characterize social welfare organization—they can pool their knowledge, bring out differences of viewpoint, and devise new or modified programs and proposals. Through social action programs they can put their facts and their proposals before those who make social policy, whether in the arena of government, the economy, or organized voluntary association. All of these methods are being increasingly used by welfare agencies at this time in a reviving recognition that their responsibility is not only to individuals but to society itself.

The Challenge Ahead

The future of America's children will be determined by institutional adaptations that go far beyond the scope of social welfare. Will a rule of law replace armed might as the instrument of international relations or will we choose to revert to the caveman's level of social organization? Will equilibrium between the world's population and its productive capacity be reached at a level of well-being for all or in a holocaust of struggle for the resources of survival? Social welfare can anticipate no role in the latter alternatives for its values are tied to a complex level of social organization and a productive capacity well above survival limits. Its own contribution to a secure future lies rather in the third area of contemporary challenge: the values represented in the social relationships among people and between individuals and their social institutions. If in the name of economic efficiency our society should sacrifice its capacity to produce responsible individuals who so shape and order their own institutions as to meet the full needs—social and spiritual, as well as economic—of all its people, including its children, then it will destroy itself from within as other civilizations have done before it. If, on the other hand, the symptoms of social maladjustment that today confront us are transitional, pointing the way to a higher plan of adaptation, social welfare must play a more creative and spirited role in moving our society toward this goal.

THE GOVERNMENT'S ROLE IN CHILD AND FAMILY WELFARE

by EVELINE M. BURNS

ALTHOUGH it is generally accepted that the family is our basic social institution and that it has primary responsibility for the well-being of its members, and in particular for the well-being of children, all modern countries have found it necessary to support the efforts of the family by action on the part of government.

This development has taken place for several reasons. First, the economic ability of the family to provide for the basic physical needs of children is conditional upon the ability of the family head to earn, without interruption, an adequate income. In our present-day economy this is not always possible. Governments have responded in various ways. Social security systems, usually consisting of some combination of social insurance and public assistance programs, are by now universal in all highly developed societies. Other efforts include minimum wage laws, vocational rehabilitation, training, assistance to families to move from depressed

Eveline M. Burns is Professor of Social Work at the New York School of Social Work, Columbia University.

areas, and broader measures to raise the levels of employment and productivity in distressed areas themselves.

A second set of considerations leading to government action in the interests of children and families has been the inability of some families to meet the basic emotional needs of children. When this happens governments step in in the interest of the child and may remove him from his own home and provide other care for him. At one time this alternative care took the form of placement in an institution, more recently, of placement in foster homes. There is, too, a new emphasis on early permanent planning for children which has led, among other things, to an increased stress on adoption. Other efforts include the provision of homemaker services, or casework and counseling with the child and his parents, or day care centers and similar facilities.

A third stimulus to governmental action stems from the fact that some actions of individuals and families may not always be in the best interests of society as a whole. For example, if the decision is left to their parents, some children, for economic or other family reasons, may not receive an education of the level that is necessary if they are to function as responsible and effective producers and as voting citizens in a democratic society. Therefore, compulsory education up to certain ages has been instituted and, to overcome the financial obstacles, this level of education has normally been provided at public expense. Or, economic pressures may lead some families to require that children work and contribute to family income. Hence we find child labor laws. Or, the way in which individuals spend their incomes when left to their own devices may not always be in the best interests of society as a whole, and laws prohibiting the sale of narcotics to all and intoxicating liquor to minors are necessary.

Finally, government, acting as the implementing agent of a democratic society, has undertaken certain functions bearing directly on the welfare of the family. National defense, a police and court system, environmental health are some of these functions. Moreover, in addition to education, which has already been mentioned, governments make available in varying degrees such commodities or services as low-income housing, medical care and rehabilitation, school lunches, free holiday transport for mothers and children, and the like. And recently it has been seen that many recreation needs, whose satisfaction involves the provision of parks, playgrounds, and large unspoiled natural areas, can be satisfied only if government takes a major responsibility for their provision.

Government's Role, 1950–1960

INCOME SECURITY. By the time of the 1950 White House Conference state and city governments were playing an important role in child and family welfare. In this chapter we shall concentrate primarily, although not exclusively, on the social security and the welfare programs as generally understood.

By 1950 the Old Age and Survivors Insurance program covered some 35 million persons by a system which, in return for the payment of social security taxes by employers and their workers throughout their working life, made available monthly payments of a predetermined amount (varying with the recipient's previous earnings) to retired workers aged sixty-five and over and to the survivors of covered workers. But the payments were low (the average monthly benefit for a single worker in 1949 was only $26.50, for a worker and aged wife $41.40 and for a widow with three children only $54.00) and many millions of families lacked any such protection because the breadwinner was employed in "uncovered employment."

In the intervening ten years the contribution of the program to family well-being has been vastly increased as a result of a series of amendments. First, coverage has been extended (notably by the amendments of 1950 and 1954) so that today 9 out of 10 jobs are covered. Second, benefits have been increased, not only for future beneficiaries but also for those on the rolls at the time the changes were made. In addition, it has been made possible to exclude 5 years of low earnings when calculating the benefit amount and to disregard all years of no earnings due to disability. These changes have led to a sizable increase in average benefits. By January, 1959, the average monthly benefit awarded to single aged workers had increased to $67.50, that for a man and eligible wife to $119.40, and that for a widow with three children to $171.70.

Third, a new risk area has been provided for. Since 1956 totally and permanently disabled workers, fifty years of age or over, have been entitled to social insurance benefits, and since 1958 their dependents have also been able to claim benefits. Of special interest to children was the 1956 amendment which provided that if a child of a deceased worker was totally physically or mentally disabled prior to reaching the age of eighteen, he could continue to receive his orphan's benefit until death, instead of losing it at age eighteen.

In contrast to the amendments of the OASDI program, which have so greatly enhanced economic security of families and children, changes in other social insurance programs during the 1950–60 decade have been either insignificant or have failed to adjust the programs to changing economic conditions. For the individuals affected by unemployment (who have averaged between 1.9 and 3.4 millions annually during this period and reached 5.4 million at the peak) unemployment insurance is a major potential resource. Coverage of this program was extended to include firms employing four workers or more by an amendment to federal law in 1954 but the states covering all employees increased only from sixteen to eighteen during this decade. Benefit amounts have been raised in most of the states but in general have failed to keep pace with rising wages: as a result the ratio which they bear to a worker's previous wages has fallen far below the 50 percent which was the objective when the system was inaugurated, in all except six states, averaging for the nation as a whole only a little more than a third of weekly wages. Of more serious concern to families is the absence of legislation providing benefits for dependents; the states with such provisions increased only to eleven at the end of 1958 as against five in 1949.

Duration of benefit has been increased in most states during this period; yet in 1958 the number of workers exhausting such benefits as their state laws entitled them to became so large that the federal government enacted a Temporary Unemployment Compensation Act to assist the states in paying benefits beyond the normal duration. Not all states took advantage of this legislation, which in any case expired in mid-1959.

In the last ten years no state has followed the example of the four which by 1950 had enacted temporary disability laws: the existing laws have however been frequently amended and are somewhat more liberal than they were.

Special categories of families such as veterans and railroad employees benefit from special income security programs. Both of these have been significantly liberalized in the last decade.

Despite the remarkable expansion of social insurance protection of families against various risks to continuity of income, the incomplete coverage of some programs and the gaps in risk coverage of the system as a whole mean that many millions of families whose sources of income have temporarily or permanently dried up must still be supported by public assistance. During 1950 there were more than 8 million persons drawing social insurance and related benefits of one kind or another. By March, 1959, the corresponding number had grown to over 20 million. Yet in the same period the number of persons receiving public assistance had increased from 5.5 million to over 6.5 million. Of these public assistance cases in 1959, 2.9 million were receiving Aid to Dependent Children payments, while about half of the 480,000 persons receiving general relief had children (averaging 2.9 per case with children).

During the ten years that have elapsed since the last White House Conference significant improvements have taken place in public assistance. Of direct concern to children was the broadening of federal aid in the Aid to Dependent Children program in 1950.

In this ten-year period amendments to the Social Security Act have considerably liberalized the federal grants to the categorical public assistance program, so that the federal share in the cost of all types of assistance has risen from 45.1 percent in 1950 to 50.4 percent in 1958. Particularly noteworthy were the changes enacted in 1958 whereby the states were given more flexibility in adjusting the size of grants in individual cases without prejudicing the extent of federal reimbursement and whereby a beginning was made, through the variable grant principle, in providing relatively more federal aid to the poorer states. Since 1956, too, the more liberal grant-in-aid arrangements have fostered the provision of more adequate medical care for public assistance recipients. But while average monthly assistance payments have increased much of this has been offset by rising prices.

Yet a third major step forward in public assistance must be noted. The amendments of 1956 radically revised the concept of the purpose of public assistance by extending government's responsibility for assurance to eligible needy persons of cash payments, needed medical care, and various services. These services are to help aged recipients attain self-care, to help the blind and the disabled to attain self-support or self-care, and in the case of recipients of Aid to Dependent Children, to help maintain and strengthen family life and help parents or relatives "to attain the maximum self-support and personal independence consistent with the maintenance of continuing parental care and protection." Although it is too soon to assess the full impact of this broadening of the objectives of public assistance, the first reports of the states to the Social Security Administration of the services they are rendering and of steps they are taking to utilize to the maximum other community agencies providing similar services suggest that the amendment has already had a stimulating effect.

But a major stumbling block has not been removed. The 1956 amendments, which so greatly broadened the responsibilities of public welfare, quite logically included authorization for additional federal money to train more personnel and to undertake needed research, but to date Congress has not voted the authorized appropriations.

In contrast to the developments that have taken place in the categorical assistance programs, little has happened in general assistance (or relief). No federal aid is available for this program and in many areas of the country it is non-existent or highly restrictive.

SPECIAL SERVICES FOR CHILDREN. During the last decade, social services developed specifically for children have in general failed to keep pace with the growth in both the child population and the increasing wealth of the country. The stimulus to the development of child welfare programs through federal grants provided under Title V of the Social Security Act has been intensified by increases in authorizations and appropriations. Yet, although the former have risen from \$3.5 million in 1949–50 to \$17 million in 1959–60 and the latter from \$3.5 million to \$13 million, it is noteworthy that after 1949–50 smaller sums have been appropriated than were authorized, and in most years the states utilized less than the sums appropriated by Congress. Moreover, the number of children served by public child welfare programs has not kept pace with the increase in the child population, falling from 55 to 51 per 10,000 children between 1946 and 1957. The decline has been particularly noteworthy in urban states where the proportion served fell from 62 to 49 per 10,000 children during this period. Only in the rural states has the percentage served increased (from 40 to 63 per 10,000 children), a situation which reflects the preference given to rural areas in the distribution of federal funds. Recognition was given to the needs of urban areas, both metropolitan and suburban, by an amendment in 1958 which eliminated the references in the allocation formula to predominantly rural areas and areas of special need.

Furthermore, only limited progress was made during the last decade in improving the caliber of staff in the public child welfare programs. Although between 1950 and 1955 the number of child welfare workers with professional degrees rose from 19 to 28 percent of the total, there remained 33 percent who had had only some graduate study and 39 percent who had none at all in an accredited school of social work.

OTHER SOCIAL WELFARE PROGRAMS. In the public programs, other than those concerned with income maintenance, less progress can be reported for the decade 1950–60. (Because programs dealing with health fall within the scope of another chapter in these volumes, no mention is here made of the notable developments of public and publicly subsidized programs in the field of health.) Although the Housing Act of 1949 offered the promise of a revised and much enlarged low-rent program by authorizing federal loans and contributions for not over 810,000 additional dwelling units over a six-year period, subsequent legislation severely cut the number of dwellings to be initiated each year. From 1950 to 1957 inclusive, only 238,000 low rent public housing units were started. In 1956 less than 5,000 units were started.

Among the more narrowly protective services, too, there was only limited progress. The minimum wage rate under the Fair Labor Standards Act was increased from 75 cents to $1.00 an hour in 1955. But efforts to raise the minimum to a level more in keeping with current price levels have been unsuccessful and the gap in federal legislation has not been filled by action on the part of the states.

Since 1950 there have been no legislative changes in the child-labor provisions of the Fair Labor Standards Act. Amendments that became effective in 1950, notably modifying the agricultural exemption, have resulted in getting more children off farms and into school. Between 1951 and 1958 school enrollment of rural youth, ten to fifteen years of age, rose from 86 to 94 percent while the urban rate remained stable at about 98 percent.

The Future Role of Government

That government, in the interest of the community as a whole, should take action on behalf of children is clearly no longer questioned. The realistic issues today concern rather the scope of that action, the specific policies to be applied, and the effectiveness of the measures adopted.

To a significant degree the role of government with regard to children has shifted from the narrower "police" function of protecting the community from the delinquent child and of protecting the helpless and neglected child from those (parents, employers, or institutions) who would take advantage of him, to a wider concept. The modern view of the use of government increasingly emphasizes developmental and positive (as opposed to narrowly protective) action and focuses more upon the child as a member of a family group than as an isolated individual. This approach broadens the potential role of government: public policy in the interest of children no longer is restricted to "child welfare services" as such but embraces all governmental measures affecting the well-being of all American families.

The precise role of government during the coming decades will depend primarily on three major considerations: first, the extent to which social, economic, and demographic developments create problems for the family which the family alone and unaided cannot resolve to the satisfaction of the community; second, the extent to which nongovernmental supra-family organizations or associations can deal effectively with the situation independently of government help, and, finally, the extent to which the nation as a whole evidences both a concern about the existence of such problems and a willingness to pay the price in terms of the money, time, and effort needed to develop suitable solutions.

The social stresses facing the family in the years immediately ahead fall into two groups: those which arise out of developments in the past for which social provision, although well under way, is not yet complete, and those which can be expected to arise as a result of more recent social, economic, and demographic changes, some of whose effects can already be predicted.

In the first group it is evident that the need for income security has not yet been fully met. The widely expressed preference for social insurance as the technique for assuring family and individual economic security has not yet been fully implemented. Coverage for unemployment insurance is far from complete. Workmen's compensation laws, also limited in coverage, have lagged far behind the newer social insurance programs. Benefits of all social insurance programs (and notably of unemployment insurance) have not kept up with rising wages and prices and call for constant scrutiny and revision. For the millions dependent for their incomes on public assistance, the situation is even more unsatisfactory. Most disturbing of all, in view of the nation's expressed concern for the welfare of its children, is the disadvantageous position of the 2.25 million children who are supported by the Aid to Dependent Children program. Because federal aid for this program has from the beginning been much less liberal than for the other categories (matching only up to $30 per child as against $65 per person in the other programs), the monthly payments per child ($28.68 in March, 1959) fall far below even the modest payment to the aged ($64.34), the disabled ($63.66), and the blind ($68.86). Furthermore, the limitation of the payment to

children in families where the father is dead, absent from
the home, or disabled, means that many needy children are
denied public aid, especially in those states that deny public
assistance to employable persons and in those where general assistance is grossly inadequate. In some cases the program operates to perpetuate or even encourage family
break-up as the only way to secure public aid.

Nor does the ADC program embody any consistent social
policy. Supposedly developed in order that the mother
would not have to seek employment and thus would be able
to remain at home to provide care for her children, the payments are almost nowhere adequate enough to remove all
inducement to the mother (and sometimes the children)
to seek paid employment. Indeed, in some communities
pressure is put on the mother to do precisely this. And if it
be the case that children need a sense of stability then the
ADC program must again be held lacking: not only may
payments be reduced from time to time on account of inadequate appropriations but eligibility for them may be en-
dangered by action by the mother which runs counter to
certain requirements, or the amount may be reduced by the
extent of earnings so that no incentive to independence
remains.

Public policy has indeed recognized the special need for
services to children. But despite the stimulus given by federal grants since 1935 to the development of child welfare
services, by 1959 almost half of the counties in the nation,
accounting for a quarter of all children, had no fulltime
public child welfare workers.

Furthermore, despite the growing emphasis on the importance of preventing family breakdown and enabling the child to remain in his own home, over 70 percent of the resources devoted to child welfare services are still spent on foster care. In December, 1957, only 38 percent of the children receiving casework services from state and local public welfare agencies were in their own homes as against 62 percent who were in foster homes, institutions, or elsewhere, and the figures for voluntary welfare agencies were much the same. Even more disconcerting is the fact that between 1946 and 1957 the number of children receiving service (unrelated to financial assistance) in their own homes increased by only 22 percent whereas those in foster homes increased by 37 percent.

Inadequate as the provision for constructive and rehabilitative services to children is as such, the status of corresponding provision for adults and families is even more unsatisfactory. We have no measure of the extent of this type of service rendered to the 5 to 6 million recipients of public assistance but all the evidence points to the fact that it is small. In some communities, public assistance recipients do not even receive the minimum physical care and medical attention to render them self-supporting. The major public rehabilitation program, Vocational Rehabilitation, as late as 1958, rehabilitated only 74,317 people annually plus another 18,584 persons who had been prepared for employment but had not found jobs. The insignificance of these figures is revealed when it is pointed out that there are estimated to be some 2 million handicapped persons who could be rehabilitated and that every year a quarter of a million persons become in need of vocational rehabilitation services.

Vocational counseling services for young people in schools and public employment agencies are still very inadequate and will become more so during the coming decade when the population expansion of the postwar years begins to affect the labor market, unless vigorous steps to expand these facilities are taken.

The gaps and inadequacies so far discussed are "unfinished business." They indicate the extent to which the nation, by 1960, had succeeded in grappling with the threats to family and child welfare due to social and economic developments of the past. But as we look ahead, it is clear that the impact on some or all families of problems created by recent developments, of trends even now evident, will call for further social provision.

One significant social change is the increasing tendency of mothers to work. In the ten years, 1948–58, the number of mothers in the labor force increased by 80 percent and the proportion of all mothers who work, by almost 50 percent. Many of these are mothers of preschool children. While fewer of these mothers work full-time (16 percent of those with preschool children as against one-third of those with older children), this still means that a problem of assuring adequate care during the mother's absence exists for a large proportion of the 3.6 million preschool children whose mothers were in the labor force in 1957.

Group day-care centers present themselves as one type of facility which might be developed to meet this need. A nationwide study conducted in May, 1958, showed that nearly 400,000 children under age twelve had to care for themselves while the mother worked and 138,000 of these children were less than ten years old. Among children under twelve with working mothers, 1 child in 13 had to look after himself for varying periods, and in the age group ten to eleven, 1 child in 5 was without any care while the mother was at work. Over a million children were looked after by nonrelatives.[1]

The inadequacy of the facilities for day-time care of children of working mothers serves only to throw into relief the larger problem of society's failure, as yet, to provide appropriate arrangements for the care of children when parents are unable to carry out their normal functions for whatever reason. While some of these arrangements may be institutional in character (day-care centers, nursery schools, school lunch programs, etc.), others involve the rendering of services in the home. In the last decade increasing attention has been devoted to homemaker services. Yet despite the great potentialities of this form of family aid, in the spring of 1958 there were only 143 agencies (serving 2,188 families) providing homemaker services, all but 33 being private agencies.

Arrangements for substitute care of children in groups or in the home may be provided on a commercial basis or by public or private welfare agencies either free or on a fee basis. Experience has shown the necessity for licensing and supervision of commercially operated services. Private agency-

[1] See the forthcoming study by the Children's Bureau, *Child Care Arrangements of Full-time Working Mothers.*

operated services are growing, but slowly, and serve primarily low-income groups. If the need is to be adequately met an expansion of public activity seems inevitable.

Another development which bears upon the role of government is the upward trend of family breakdown in the nation as a whole. On the one hand more babies are being born out of wedlock; on the other hand, there appears to be an increase in the break-up of marriages and more divorces involve children. In 1956, the illegitimacy rate of unmarried women aged fifteen to forty-four (20.2 per 1,000) was almost three times as high as in 1940 and such births constituted 4.65 percent of total live births as against 3.79 in 1940. And although the proportion of illegitimate births accounted for by teen-agers has declined (40 percent in 1956 as against almost 50 percent in 1940), and despite the trend to earlier marriage, 1 in 7 of all girls fifteen to nineteen years of age who bore a child was not married.

The divorce rate per 1,000 married women, although far less than its postwar peak of 17.8, is still above that of 1940 (9.2 in 1957 as against 8.8 in 1940) and in 1958 the number of married women who reported themselves as separated from their husbands was nearly as great as the number reporting themselves divorced. And with the trend to earlier marriages and earlier child bearing, more of the divorces involve children. About half of the divorces granted in 1956 were to couples with at least one child under eighteen and 1 in 9 divorcing couples had as many as three children.[2]

[2] The data in these paragraphs are derived from "Facts about Families," *Social Security Bulletin* (May, 1959), pp. 9–14.

As against these developments, only one cheerful fact can be noted: full orphanhood is on the way out. As a result of improvements in medical science and social protective measures, fewer women die in childbirth and fewer workers die because of industrial accidents or occupational diseases. By 1957 the number of orphans with both parents dead was estimated to be only 55,000, while there were 1,890,000 with the father dead and 800,000 with the mother dead.

Public recognition of the fact that the social problems of dependent children are primarily problems of broken homes rather than orphanhood has come slowly. Great progress has been made in devising social measures to protect the economic welfare of the orphan, primarily as a result of the OASDI program. But against this effective provision for the economic needs of the orphan, social provision for the equally large number of children affected by broken homes has lagged. In 1956 it was estimated that some 2.5 million children lived with the mother in a broken home and some 200,000 children lived with their father only. Hitherto public provision for the economic needs of such children has taken the form of Aid to Dependent Children, which has increasingly become a "broken families" program as OASDI has shouldered more and more of the responsibility for the orphaned child. At the end of 1958, 59.8 percent of the fathers in ADC families were divorced or separated or had deserted the family or were not married to the mother. This preponderance of broken families, together with the sharp upward trend of ADC recipients (from 599,000 families and 1.52 million children in 1949 to 775,600 families and 2.24

million children in March, 1959), has exposed the program to much adverse criticism.

Some of this criticism is uninformed, and fails to take account of the facts cited above relative to the trends of divorce, separation, and illegitimacy in the nation as a whole and of the increased child population. Furthermore, it seems probable that part of the remarkable increase in broken families in receipt of ADC reflects the fact that when government accepts financial responsibility for the support of certain precisely defined categories of persons their true number becomes known for the first time (just as the number of disabled children under eighteen qualifying for OASDI benefits exceeded the estimates made before benefits became available to them in 1956). It is highly probable that before the days of ADC there were large numbers of broken families living below public assistance levels, but no statistical count was made of them. Unfortunately, too, public attention focuses on the inadequate parents and not on the hundreds of thousands of ADC mothers who make a decent home for their children despite shockingly inadequate monthly payments. Yet even when allowance is made for these facts, it remains true that family breakdown has now to be recognized as a major cause of income insecurity among children.

Popular resentment of the large numbers and steady growth of the broken home ADC recipients has led to actions which gravely jeopardize the welfare of children. Sometimes efforts are made to refuse payments after a second or third illegitimate child is born, or to force the mother to seek paid work, or to remove the child from the family. Elsewhere, the low level of ADC monthly payments per recipient probably reflects the general disparagement of this category. The effect upon these children, who will be the citizens of tomorrow, of meager and uncertain living standards, and of social disapproval, denied as they are in any case the benefit of normal two-parent home environment, seems often to be forgotten in the concern of communities to keep down illegitimacy and dependency rates.

All this is not to deny that the broken home has become a major social problem calling for more knowledge of its causes and more constructive and imaginative programs for its prevention and control. Hitherto society has attempted to discharge its responsibilities through a single program, ADC, providing a meager income and limited casework service, supplemented by a very inadequate system of specialized public and private child welfare services. No greater challenge faces a nation professedly concerned with the well-being of children than a reassessment of social policy in relation to the broken home. Such a reassessment would have to place much greater stress on prevention. It would explore more imaginatively the contribution that could be made by organizations and institutions additional to courts, correctional agencies, and those now thought of as "welfare agencies," such as the schools, the churches, trade unions, and the like. Above all, it would be postulated upon the assumptions that the major concern is to strengthen the family and the major test of achievement is the welfare of the child.

A third development pointing to a larger role for government is the fact that during the last ten years the average American family has become steadily better off. The median money income for all families from all sources rose from $2,530 in 1944 to $4,970 in 1957. Even after allowing for price increases and the higher tax rates of recent years, this is a sizable improvement. As the general level of economic well-being rises, it throws into relief the position of groups who have not shared in the general prosperity. The number of families of whom this is true is disturbingly large.[3]

The disparity in average per capita income between the richest and the poorest states is still great, ranging as it does from $968 in Mississippi and $1,122 in Arkansas to $2,744 in Delaware and $2,678 in Connecticut in 1955–57. In the poorer states not only are average family incomes much lower, but the ability of the community at large to support needed public or private welfare services is restricted. Families who derive their living from agriculture have also failed to keep pace with the general prosperity.[4] The median money income for rural farm families in 1954 was only $1,973. Furthermore, agricultural workers are currently excluded from most governmental protective legislation, such

[3] For the facts about low-income families, see U.S. Congress, Joint Committee on the Economic Report, *Characteristics of the Low-Income Population and Related Federal Programs*, 1955; *and Low-Income Families*, Hearings before the Sub-Committee on Low-Income Families, 84th Cong., 2nd Sess. (Washington: G.P.O., 1955); and the series of reports issued by the New York State Interdepartmental Committee on Low Incomes.

[4] For a vivid account of the living and working conditions of agricultural wage-earning families, see *Report on Farm Labor* (New York: National Advisory Committee on Farm Labor, 1959).

as the Fair Labor Standards Act, Unemployment Insurance, Workmen's Compensation, the Taft-Hartley Act, and Child Labor Laws. Most disadvantaged of all are the 380,000 American migrant workers and their families, while the approximately 500,000 foreign migrant workers in agriculture, although in most cases given more protection through agreements with their national governments, are almost as badly off. The migrant family has low and uncertain income, unsatisfactory housing, inadequate health facilities, and, in some communities, limited access to social services because of its "nonresident" status. The child in the migrant family frequently works in the fields with his parents, he suffers from inadequate and interrupted schooling, and he and his family lack the sense of stability and security that comes from a feeling of "belonging" to any community.

The average level of incomes of minority groups, notably Negroes, Puerto Ricans, and Mexicans, also falls below the general average: their housing conditions are less favorable, their educational levels are lower, and their health records are poorer than those of the general population.

In general children who are members of large families have also failed to share in the general prosperity. Income increases as the size of the family increases only up to the point where there are two children in the family. Thereafter, income actually decreases quite rapidly as the family size grows. In 1954 the median income of the two-child family was $4,506 while that of the five-child family was only $3,155, with three extra people to support. It has been estimated that whereas only 14.8 percent of all families with two children in 1954 had annual money incomes equal to less than half the city worker's family budget, 19.4 percent of three-children families, 31.7 percent of four-children families, 47.8 percent of five-children families, and over 51.8 percent of families with six or more children were in this situation. (The city worker's family budget is a measure of the dollar cost of maintaining a family of a specified size at a level of living which meets prevailing standards of health, efficiency, nurture of children, and participation in community activities. It describes a "modest but adequate," rather than a "luxury" or "subsistence" standard.) When it is recalled that 54 percent of the nation's children are in families with three or more children, these facts give rise to serious concern.

Finally, all those families or individuals dependent on socially provided income, whether social insurance or public assistance, constitute another large segment of the population who have failed to keep pace with the general rise in living standards.

Many of the measures needed to ensure all American families a level of living in keeping with current standards of adequacy and consistent with our steadily increasing national product necessitate action by both government and the individual citizen, such as measures to eliminate discrimination. Others are of a kind that only governments can take. They include extension of minimum wage laws and laws governing the employment of children to cover all employments and all children. They call for federal aid to the poorer states greater in proportion to that given to the richer in order that families dwelling therein may not be denied access to the commonly accepted level and range of social services.

They suggest both assistance to families to move away from depressed areas to others of greater opportunity and also aid to revitalize certain depressed areas. They call for the extension of educational opportunity and training and vocational guidance facilities for all children, for all studies demonstrate that as a group the low-income families are characterized by poor education and lack of skills, and their position will become even more disadvantaged as automation and advanced technology create greater demands for well-educated and skilled workers. They include revision of our social security programs to ensure that benefits keep pace not only with prices but also with the rise in average standards of living. They may even involve the adoption of some system of children's allowances or other special aids to members of large families to offset the disadvantages suffered by children therein, for the only current public policy in the interests of large families, income tax exemptions for children, helps only those families who would normally pay sizable taxes and in any case does not put any additional money into the homes with the lowest incomes.[5]

All signs point to a continuance of the high mobility of the American population and even to some increase of the

[5] It has been estimated that the percentages of families with incomes of less than the tax exemptions to which they were entitled in 1954 were: families with one child, 14.6 percent; two children, 16.6 percent; three children, 25.5 percent; four children, 44.5 percent; five children, 66.6 percent; six or more children, over 76.9 percent. James C. Vadakin, *Family Allowances* (Miami: University of Miami Press, 1958), p. 163.

rate as the shift of families from the cities to the suburban areas gathers momentum. The need for adequate community facilities in both the city and its suburbs is thereby intensified. In the newer communities, facilities have to be brought into existence. The older cities face even more serious problems due to the draining away both of the better-off families who seek the living amenities of the suburbs and of business enterprises seeking lower costs of operation outside the highly taxed or high-rent cities. Thus they are being left with a population that in general is poorer and more likely to be in need of social services including, notably, subsidized housing and community facilities, while at the same time their tax base has shrunk. Unless the cities and the families remaining within them are to suffer progressive deterioration and "urban blight," there will have to be more extensive and vigorous public action in the form of urban renewal, public housing, development of recreational facilities, and the like.

The broadening of objectives in housing policy to include urban renewal has created new and challenging problems such as the relocation of tenants from the condemned areas, and the provision of adequate and well-coordinated community facilities and services in the redeveloped areas. In addition, it is increasingly realized that the provision of satisfactory housing for the nation's families is not assured merely by making available "decent, safe, and sanitary dwellings." Underprivileged families from the slums need help in raising their standards and adjusting to new conditions. And the problem is complicated by the fact that existing income limits as a condition of eligibility tend to make the housing project a concentration of low income groups, among whom public assistance recipients (and notably ADC mothers) and minority groups form, inevitably, a large proportion.

The Contribution of Non-Governmental Institutions

Whether or not these developments, which affect the well-being of some or all children in varying degrees, will, in fact, lead to an expanded role for government will depend in part on the extent to which other social institutions are interested in, or are able to take, action which is beyond the power of the individual family. For our society is characterized by the existence of a large number of voluntary associations formed by individuals or families to deal with certain problems that no one family or individual could deal with alone and un-aided. Workers have formed trade unions, which have fought not merely for higher wages but in recent years also for various guarantees of income after earning ceases or for group provision of services needed by all families even when earning power is not interrupted. Many millions of families and their children benefit today from such privately nego-tiated benefits as retirement pensions, supplementary unem-ployment compensation, health insurance, and the like. But spectacular as has been the growth of these arrangements in recent years, they cannot substitute for governmental pro-grams. First, not all families have breadwinners who are employed in highly organized industries, and these include many of the families most in need of help or protection.

Such additional benefits, over and above decent wages, are typically not found in agriculture, or in small firms, or in struggling industries. Second, even where such programs exist they do not do the whole job: they are additional to the basic provision by government. It is significant both that their great growth has followed the assumption by government of responsibility for assuring basic minimum security, and that they are known as "fringe" benefits.

Families also combine with others to deal with common problems in other areas. Since World War II, there has been a remarkable growth of associations initiated by parents of children with specific physical or mental disabilities. But while some of these organizations have succeeded in raising sizable sums of money to finance research and other programs of their own, it is significant that a considerable fraction of their energies is directed to exerting pressure on governments to make special provision in school systems, health services, and the like for the children whose interests they represent.

Private philanthropy is another institution which supplements the ability of families to deal with social and economic problems and which at one time was in a very real sense an alternative to government action. But some of the problems today are of such magnitude and involve the raising of such large sums of money as to be beyond the capacity of even the most generously supported private welfare organizations. The function of assuring basic economic security is now generally agreed to be one that government, rather than private philanthropy should assume for this very reason. Indeed, leading private welfare agencies now vigorously support more adequate governmental income security programs on the ground that unless government accepts this responsibility the private agencies cannot carry out their own responsibilities. But in other areas, too, private welfare is no longer seen as an alternative to government but rather as carrying out certain functions which, for religious, cultural, or other reasons are believed to be more appropriately performed by nongovernmental bodies.

One area in which private welfare has played a very important role is the provision of casework services to children. Yet even here, in June, 1957, in the country as a whole, of about 404,000 children receiving casework services, public agencies were giving primary service to about 281,000 children and secondary services to another 50,000 served primarily by private agencies, while the latter were giving primary service to about 123,000 and secondary services to another 2,000. Thus public agencies were serving 43 children per 10,000 child population while the private agencies were serving 19. These figures exclude most of the children in families receiving public assistance some of whom undoubtedly receive governmental services, and also those receiving services directly from juvenile courts and probation departments. Inclusion of such children would still further increase the preponderance of the public sector. Furthermore, in some cases, although the private agencies were rendering services, their cost was met wholly or in some degree by government.[6] To the extent this occurs, sponsorship ceases to be purely "private" as opposed to "public," for decisions as to the extent of subsidization and the desirability of providing services indirectly through private agencies rather than directly by government move into the realm of public policy.

The role of voluntary welfare is dealt with more extensively in another chapter in this volume. Here we are concerned only with the extent to which private philanthropy can realistically be regarded as an alternative to government in grappling with the major social problems facing families in the coming decades. All the evidence suggests that its role can only be that of an important supplement although it will inevitably be greater in some functional areas than others. In 1955, for example, private agency expenditures for family and other child welfare services were a little more than 3 times as large as the corresponding public expenditures (excluding services rendered under the public assistance programs). But the inadequate and underdeveloped state of these services throughout most of the country and the many unmet needs for additional services caution against any inference that the vastly greater sums needed to equip the country with an acceptable volume and level of service could be secured from private philanthropy. Between 1945

[6] Slightly over 43 percent of all payments for foster care by state and local public welfare agencies were payments for children in homes or institutions supervised or administered by voluntary agencies. *Child Welfare Statistics, 1957*, Children's Bureau Statistical Series 51, Social Security Administration, U. S. Dept. of Health, Education, and Welfare, 1959, p. 26. In 1952 the United Community Funds and Councils reported that 12.5 percent of the total income of voluntary services providing specialized services for children came from public funds.

and 1955 expenditures from philanthropic contributions for health and welfare purposes (excluding education and religious purposes) are estimated to have increased from $1.2 billion to $1.9 billion. During the same period the corresponding public expenditures rose from $8.1 billion to $22.2 billion.[7]

The Degree of Citizen Concern

The extent to which the people of the United States will be willing to make use of the instrument of government to implement the pledges made to their children at the 1950 White House Conference will depend upon their willingness to pay the necessary price in money, time, and effort. It must be recognized at once that the money price, in terms of the additional tax monies needed, will be stiff. It will be necessary to devote a larger proportion of national income to these social programs if existing deficiencies are to be made good and if even a modest effort is to be made to grapple with the newer problems created by current economic, social, and demographic developments. Moreover this social provision will have to be made for a rapidly growing number of children. Between 1950 and 1958 the number of children under eighteen increased from 47.0 million to 61.3 million, and it is expected to increase to 79.0 million in 1970.

But increased tax revenues do not necessarily mean proportionately increased tax rates. How much incomes avail-

[7] For data on public social welfare expenditures, see Ida Merriam "Social Welfare in the United States, 1934–54," *Social Security Bulletin* (October, 1955), pp. 2ff., and "Social Welfare Expenditures in the United States, 1956–57," *ibid.* (October, 1958), pp. 22ff.

able for private spending would be reduced by additional
expenditures on governmental programs in the interests of
children and families will depend upon the rate of growth
of national productivity. In the recent past, national product
has been increasing at the rate of 3 to 3.5 percent a year. It
is this increase which accounts for the fact that although
public social welfare expenditures for all purposes (including
education) have risen from $7.8 billion in 1936–37, to $16.5
billion in 1946–47 and to 37.9 billion in 1956–57, we are
still devoting a smaller percentage of our total economic
output to such ends (8.8 percent in 1956–57 as against 8.9
percent twenty years earlier). It is this rise of productivity,
too, which has enabled the average income receiver to dis-
pose, as he wishes, of a steadily rising income even after payment of all taxes for social welfare, defense, and other purposes. Current estimates suggest that in the years immediately ahead at least this rate of economic progress can be
anticipated and some authorities put it even higher. (The
National Planning Association uses an average of 4.2 percent as the most probable figure.) To the extent that these
forecasts are borne out, the burden of financing more adequate public social welfare services (in the widest sense)
will be lightened. Nor must it be forgotten that many types
of social welfare expenditure result in additions to the nation's productive potential or save other costs. The disabled
worker who is rehabilitated, the child who secures a better
education, the family which is helped to attain self-support,
yield economic returns for the public investment in them.
And the families which are prevented from breaking up, or

the child who is saved from delinquency represent a saving in social costs in future years.

Even so, it would be unrealistic not to expect that effective development of publicly provided goods and services will require the devotion of a larger proportion of national income to these programs. Whether or not this will happen will depend upon prevailing values, on how much people care about the well-being of children and families, and how much they know about the nature of the problems and the effectiveness of the measures for dealing with them. That people are willing to spend more of their income on publicly provided goods and services when they are convinced of the worthiness of the objective and the effectiveness of the program is shown by the growth of expenditures on social insurance (from $3.86 per capita in 1936–37 to $73.37 in 1956–57). If there is an equal concern about the broken family or unsatisfactory housing, they will be willing to spend on the relevant programs more than the $4.44 and $.70 per head which they spent in 1956–57.

WORK, WOMEN, AND CHILDREN

by HENRY DAVID

THERE IS an obvious measure of truth in the frequently heard assertion that the society of the United States is strongly child-centered. No other major society in the world, for example, provides as many or as varied educational opportunities for its young. Probably no other society is as responsive to the consumption desires of its young—or to adult beliefs about what the young want and need in their pursuit of happiness. No other society allocates as large a volume of goods and services to the satisfaction of these consumption desires. Probably no other society has fashioned as elaborate and extensive a system—and this implies no judgment on its adequacy—of public and private agencies and services for dealing with the problems and needs of its children and youth.

More subtle qualitative evidences may also be invoked in support of the characterization of Americans as a child-centered people. Thus, in contrast to the peoples of other

Henry David is Executive Director of the National Manpower Council and Dean of the Graduate Faculty of Political and Social Science at the New School for Social Research.

Western societies, Americans seem to be more self-conscious in their search for and adoption of what is alleged to be the newest and, of course, the best mode of child-rearing. The market for books and periodical and newspaper articles which offer "scientific" advice on the care, rearing, and development of children at all ages is enormous. However uncertain they may be about the psychological significance of the concept, Americans seem to share a universal concern with giving their offspring a sense of "security." Currently, they seem to be dedicated to the proposition that the young should not be "frustrated" in their growing-up experiences and in their relationships with one another or with adults.

To some foreign observers these signs of a child-centered society testify to an excessive, perhaps even a neurotic, preoccupation with the young at the expense of adults. This kind of critical observation about the posture of Americans toward their children is, of course, traditional. In part, it grows out of the fact that Americans have long seemed far less disposed than other Western people to define a "place" for their children, or to act on the belief that children should have a place and be kept in it whatever "it" might be. In the nineteenth century, Anthony Trollope found it unfortunate that American children were "never banished, snubbed, and kept in the background," as children were in England. More recent European visitors have been struck by the extent to which American children participate as equals in many aspects of adult life from which the young in other societies are normally excluded. Europeans also frequently find it odd that American adults encourage their young to voice opinions on the most complex and difficult social, economic, and political issues and that they manifest respectful attention to the views that children express on these issues. One English visitor is reported to have remarked that the schools of the United States and American middle-class family life seem to be conducted according to the principle: "The child knows best."

On the surface it appears true that the world of the adult and the world of the young are less sharply differentiated in the United States than in other Western societies. It may even be argued that, since early in the nineteenth century, considerations of equality and freedom and the value placed upon early self-dependence have conspired, in combination with other influences, to blur the lines between these two worlds. The fact that years alone do not seem to establish a claim for superior status and deference, as they do in many societies, and that rigid distinctions are not maintained between the young and adults with respect to dress, patterns of social behavior, recreational activities, freedom of personal conduct, and the like, may be taken as additional marks of a child-centered society.

In spite of a preoccupation with the young, however, it also remains true that most Americans appear to have been singularly indifferent to the import that one of the major social transformations which the United States has experienced during the present century may have for the rearing and development of their children and youth. That transformation is the one which has taken place in the employment of women—more particularly in the employment of wives and mothers—outside the home. At first glance, one might expect that changes of almost revolutionary proportions in the normal pattern of women's lives and in the functions of married women would be seized upon as having far-reaching consequences for the form and substance of family life and for the care and rearing of the young. One might further expect that, in a society which values its young so highly and which is presumably so concerned with their healthy development, changes of this character would immediately stimulate serious reflection and inquiry. Neither of these expectations, however, has in fact been realized.

The scale of the change which has taken place since the close of the nineteenth century in women's employment outside the home is suggested by the following comparisons: In 1890, the Census Bureau counted about 4 million gainfully employed women who represented one-sixth of the nation's working population and the same proportion of the women in the United States aged ten and over. In the last several years, however, between 21.5 and 23 million women have been in the labor force in the course of any one month. In the course of any year, about 28 million women have been employed outside the home. In recent years, moreover, women have accounted for about 30 percent of the nation's total labor force, and about one-third of all women fourteen years and older have been employed outside the home.

The most recent United States Department of Labor data on employment show that out of a total civilian labor force of just over 70 million in October, 1959, 23.5 million—or one third—were women. In that month, better than a third of all women aged fourteen and over were employed outside the home. About 33.9 million of the 63.5 million fourteen and older—or about 54 percent—who were not in the labor force were engaged in keeping house, while another 4.7 million were attending school.

Explanations of why women have come to play so important a role in the nation's labor force require no detailed treatment here. It is sufficient to note, as the National Manpower Council remarked, that: "To make clear the variety and the complexity of the factors which have affected the demand for and the supply of women workers during the present century would require retelling the history of the United States. Growth and change in the economy, advances in science and technology, an expanding urban population, developments in education, the role of government as an employer, the crisis situations of war and depression, social values and attitudes, patterns of marriage, childbearing, and life expectancy—all have contributed significantly to the revolution in women's employment."[1]

More significant than the increases in the numbers of women employed either full time or part time outside the home, and more significant than the steep rise in the proportion of the working population accounted for by women are the changes which have taken place since the close of the nineteenth century in the age and marital characteristics of women workers. More than half of the women workers in 1890 were under twenty-five years old, and only 15 percent

[1] National Manpower Council, *Womanpower* (New York: Columbia University Press, 1957), p. 9.

of the employed women were over forty-five. In recent years however, less than one-fifth of all women workers have been under twenty-five, at least half have been more than forty years old, and almost two-fifths have been over forty-five. As late as 1940, women above forty-five accounted for only a little more than one-fifth of all women in the labor force, while those under twenty-five still constituted one third. At the turn of the century, peak participation in the labor force occurred among the twenty-year-old women, and in 1940 among women eighteen and nineteen years old. During the last several years, however, women around fifty are as likely to be in the labor force as those of any other age. Currently, about the same proportion—that is, almost half—of all the fifty-year-old women in the nation, as of all the twenty-year-old women, are engaged in work outside the home.

In October, 1959, a larger percentage (49.7) of all forty-five to fifty-four-year-old women were employed than of those in the eighteen to twenty-four year age group (47.5 percent). Moreover, labor force participation rates for women between forty-five and forty-nine ran higher than for those eighteen and nineteen years old. In that month, the actual number of women between forty-five and fifty-four who were counted as employed exceeded by almost 300,000 the number reported not in the labor force who were engaged in keeping house.

Implicit in the changes which have taken place in their age characteristics are the equally radical alterations which have occurred in the marital status of working women. Early in the century, the typical working woman was not only relatively young, but she was also single. Today, she is married. Over the last several years, the married women have accounted for 6 out of every 10 women in the labor force. At the end of the nineteenth century, while employment outside the home was common among married Negro women, it was relatively exceptional among married white women. Even though gainful employment was more common among immigrant women than among the native born whites, only 2.5 percent of the white married women in the United States in 1890 were reported by the Census as gainfully employed. Now, employment outside the home among married women is nearly as characteristic for whites as for Negroes, and is found among all socio-economic groups.

The full significance of the replacement of the single woman by the married woman in the labor force appears in the fact that for several years now better than 30 percent of all the married women in the country have been employed outside the home. Even more important from the viewpoint of the rearing and development of the young, is the fact that an even larger proportion of all the mothers of school-age children in the nation—at least 4 out of every 10— are currently found in the labor force.

Most of the striking growth in the employment of wives and mothers has come about during the last two decades. In commenting upon the participation of married women in the labor force, Simeon Strunsky, writing at the close of the 1930s, could still point out that what deserved recognition was the vastly greater number not engaged in work outside the home. Observing that some "three million married women were in gainful employment outside the home in 1930," he went on to remark: "In absolute numbers and the peculiarly intricate nature of their problem, the married women workers are obviously a major social factor of our day. Yet the married women workers are little more than ten percent of all the married women in the nation. Eight out of every nine married women still have the home as their sole economic interest. The married woman worker is a problem to herself and society, but she is not the typical married woman of the times." [2]

Now, almost one-third of all the married women living with their husbands are employed outside the home. On the other hand, less than 4 out of every 10 widowed or divorced women, as well as of the married women not living with their husbands, and less than 5 out of 10 single women are working.

Since the eve of World War II, the rise in the employment of married women has been spectacular. Thus, between 1940 and 1955, among thirty-five- to forty-four-year-old married women living with their husbands, the proportion in the labor force more than doubled. During the same period, there was almost a tripling in the proportion of married women aged forty-five to sixty-four who were employed outside the home. From 1947 to 1957 alone, participation in the labor force among married women increased by half.

A Census Bureau report noted that in March, 1957, "The number of married women in the labor force—either em-

---

[2] Simeon Strunsky, *The Living Tradition. Change and America* (New York: Doubleday, Doran, 1939), pp. 55–56.

ployed or seeking jobs—was at a record spring level of 12.7
million. . . . During the period since World War II, there
has been an average yearly increase of about one-half million
in the number of working wives." It should be noted that
only 1.2 million of the 12.7 million wives then employed
outside the home were not living with their husbands. In
March, 1957, almost one-third of the more than 50 million
women in the United States with children under eighteen
were in the labor force. Among the more than 11 million
mothers with children of school age, two-fifths were working.
At that time moreover, there were more than 2.5 million
mothers in the labor force whose children were of pre-school
age. These working wives represented 17 percent of all
mothers with pre-school children, and almost all of them
were living with their husbands.

The recession of 1957–58 did not discourage participation
in the labor force among married women. In 1958, reported
the Census Bureau, "a little over half of the women in the
labor force" were "working wives living with their husbands," and only one-fourth of the working women were
single. In March, 1958, the number of wives in the labor
force had reached a new high of 13 million, and all but 1.2
million of them were living with their husbands. It may be
noted that a tiny minority of these working wives, somewhere between 1 and 2 percent, were holding more than
one job. In March, 1958, more than 4.6 million mothers
with children between the ages of six and seventeen—or
over two-fifths of all such mothers in the nation—were employed outside the home. Moreover, one-fifth of all the

mothers with children under six were at that time counted in the labor force, and of these 2.8 million working mothers with children of pre-school age, less than half a million were living apart from their husbands, or were widowed or divorced.

In recent years, only about one-third of all the women in the labor force have been full-time workers. The other two-thirds have been either part-time or part-year employees. It is significant, therefore, that a special survey conducted in 1958 for the Children's Bureau by the Census Bureau provided fresh information on the extent of full-time employment among working mothers. The data showed that in May of that year, the mothers of some 2 million children under six years of age were full-time workers. In addition, there were about 3 million children between the ages of six and twelve whose mothers were working full time.

The rapid increase in the employment of wives and mothers outside the home in recent years may be viewed as the product of an expanding economy and of growing and changing labor force requirements, which exerted a steady high demand for women workers at a time when the supply of men workers was inadequate because of the low birth rates two decades earlier. But this is only a partial view of a development which represents a new pattern of life for women. Work outside the home normally occurred in the past during the earlier years of a woman's life. It is less than thirty years since marriage meant the withdrawal from gainful employment for most women who had worked when they were single. Generally speaking, early in the twentieth century only those who were compelled to work by economic necessity or who were motivated by strong career drives continued to remain employed after they married. Now, as has been seen, employment outside the home is a characteristic experience at two distinct stages of a woman's life— during her younger years and after marriage when her last child has reached school age.

A substantial minority of girls enter the labor force while they are still in high school, and it is customary for young women to work before they marry and even after. Rather than marriage itself, it is the first pregnancy which is likely to result in the young wife's departure from the labor force. While many mothers of very young children, as has been seen, continue to be employed outside the home, largely for compelling economic reasons, the labor force participation rates among mothers with preschool-age children are relatively low. Once their children reach school age, mothers display a strong tendency to return to the labor force or to enter it for the first time.

This tendency is shown by the rise in labor force participation for women after they reach thirty and by the fact that the proportion employed outside the home is at least twice as great among mothers with school-age children as among those with children under six. Employment increases steadily with advancing years until about age fifty, so much so that there is ground for speaking of a large-scale "return to work" movement among women in their thirties, forties, and fifties—that is, among mothers who are uncertainly described as "mature" or "older." The decline in employment

outside the home begins after fifty, but it is not until after
the sixtieth year that a significant drop in the labor force
participation rates occurs. Thus, in October, 1959, the percentage of women in the fifty-five to sixty-four-year age group
who were in the labor force was slightly larger than that
among the twenty-five to thirty-four years olds.

Of the variety of developments which have led to the
present patterning of work in the lives of women, four merit
special attention. One is the increase in the marriage rates.
According to population experts, under present conditions
less than 7 percent of American women never marry. The
extent to which Americans reject the unmarried state is revealed by the fact that the number of married couples in the
United States increased by 5.5 million during the decade beginning in 1947. Not only does a larger proportion of American women marry than in the past, but they marry at an
earlier age. Currently, half of the women in the United
States marry before they are twenty-one, and, with the exception of the small number who remain single, almost all
women marry before they reach their thirtieth birthday.

Related to early marriage is the third development
connected with the tendency for married women in their
thirties to enter or reenter the labor force. That is the reduction in the period of time within which the family is completed, even though there has also been a marked increase,
since the depressed 1930s, in the number of children per
family. Seventy years ago, when twenty-three was the median
age of marriage, half of the women had their last child when
they were thirty-two. Consequently, half of the women were

only a year or two away from forty when the youngest child entered school. Now, however, the median age of women when they bear the last child is only twenty-six, which means that their median age is thirty-two when the youngest child enters school. The earlier age of marriage, moreover, means that most women will not have reached fifty when the youngest child marries.

The fourth development, the rise in average life expectancy, has also contributed to the tendency of women in their thirties, forties, and fifties to work outside the home. Under present conditions, 3 out of every 4 women can expect to live to sixty-five, and 1 out of 4 to age eighty-five. There is now a long period of years during which mothers are relieved in greater or lesser degree from the more onerous and more time- and energy-consuming responsibilities of child care and homemaking. Average life expectancy for a woman of forty today is about seventy-six, but at the opening of the century it was only sixty-nine. A woman can now expect to live about thirteen years longer after her youngest child reaches school age than she could sixty years ago. Then she could look forward to only thirty years of life on the average after her last child entered school.

Existing patterns of work outside the home are not likely, under any series of reasonable assumptions, to alter drastically in the near future. Careful projections indicate that adult women—most of whom will be wives and mothers—will play a critical role in the anticipated expansion of the working population. Thus, U. S. Department of Labor studies estimate that "women 35 years and over will contribute over 4 million of the total labor force growth of 10½ million between 1955 and 1965. The number of women 25–34 in the labor force will probably show no change . . . ; women 20–24 will increase by about a half million because of sharply rising numbers in the population." [3] To the 13 million increase projected for the 1965–1975 decade, it is expected that adult women will also contribute significantly.

It was observed earlier that the growing employment of wives and mothers did not prompt intensive inquiries into its implications for the rearing and development of the young or for other aspects of family life. Generalizations about the feelings and behavior of Americans as a whole—or of any other people, for that matter—should always be regarded with suspicion. Nevertheless, there is ground for contending that Americans adapted to and accepted, in spite of traditional attitudes toward the "proper" functions of women, the new place which work outside the home came to occupy in the lives of married women and the new significance of wives and mothers in the labor force.

Furthermore, it is possible to argue that while some Americans may have felt that having more and more married women employed outside the home produced some socially undesirable results, or threatened men's job opportunities, most of them seemed to act as if that development was, on balance, to be welcomed. Finally, it may be stated with greater assurance that there was no great sense of urgency to discover precisely how the children and youth of the nation were being affected by the virtual revolution which had occurred in women's employment outside the home.

[3] Sophia Cooper, "Labor Force Projections to 1975," *Monthly Labor Review* (December, 1957), p. 1445.

This last observation is strongly supported by the comment made as late as 1957 by Mrs. Katherine Brownell Oettinger, Chief of the Children's Bureau, that "we do not yet have dependable research evidence, one way or the other," on "the effects of maternal employment per se" upon children.[4] A recent review of the research on children during the decade 1949–1958, reported to the Children's Bureau Clearinghouse for Research in Child Life, suggests that relatively few thoroughgoing investigations had been made into the consequences of maternal employment upon child development or upon the needs for and availability of child care and other welfare services, in the light of recent levels of participation in the labor force among younger mothers. While many Americans believe that there is a positive relationship between maternal employment and delinquency, and that the children of working mothers are badly neglected, this review of a decade's research on children underlines the paucity of reliable data on these popular generalizations. The plea for "more solid information than we now have about . . . maternal employment" as a possible cause of delinquency is frequently heard.[5] Two recent thoughtful papers [6] which deal with the relationship between the employment of mothers and child development make

[4] National Manpower Council, *Work in the Lives of Married Women* (New York: Columbia University Press, 1958), p. 141.

[5] See, for example, Catherine E. Harris, "A Decade of Research Concerning Children," *Children* (July–August, 1959), p. 148.

[6] Eleanor Maccoby, "Effects Upon Children of their Mothers' Outside Employment" in *Work in the Lives of Married Women*, pp. 150–72; John Rose, M.D., "Child Development and the Part-Time Mother," *Children* (November–December, 1959), pp. 213–18.

it clear that current knowledge in this area is not only limited but also speculative in character.

Only recently have national data become available on the means relied upon to provide care for the children of mothers employed outside the home, but not, it should be noted, on the quality of the care these children actually receive. The special Census Bureau survey mentioned earlier indicated that in May, 1958, about two-fifths of the 2 million children of pre-school age whose mothers were in the labor force "were taken care of by relatives other than their parents, including older children in some cases. Another fifth or so were looked after by their own fathers or mothers who either worked different shifts or whose working conditions were such as to permit the children to stay with them. In some cases, the mother worked at home, in family business or farms, in schools, or in other places where it was possible to keep her children with her during working hours. Roughly one-fourth of the children were cared for by neighbors or other nonrelatives while their mothers were working, but only 5 percent were placed in 'group care centers,' such as day nurseries, nursery schools, settlement houses, etc." [7]

Some 24,000 children under three and 67,000 between six and twelve, whose mothers were employed, were looked after in one fashion or another by older children in the family or by adults, but a substantial number of them were expected to care for themselves while their mothers were working. Apparently, among the ten- and eleven-year-old chil-

[7] U. S. Department of Commerce, Bureau of the Census, Current Population Reports, Series P-50 (January, 1959), p. 6.

dren, 1 out of 5 was expected to care for himself while the mother was at work.

The absence of the mother from the home is a point of major concern in many of the comments made about the effects of maternal employment upon children. And this is understandable. Not only is care of the child taken to be the primary responsibility of the mother, but it is also widely assumed that the mother's physical proximity to the child, and, therefore, her constant availability to respond to his needs, is an essential pre-condition for adequate care. Perhaps the more distinguishing features of a child-centered society are the beliefs that the healthy development of the child depends almost exclusively upon the central mother-child relationship, and that parents are ideal companions for their children. "It is a peculiarity of parents, especially of mothers," remarked Katherine Anthony many years ago, "that they never entertain a modest doubt as to whether they might be the best of all possible company for their children." [8]

It is, of course, almost self-evident that it is not so much the physical proximity of the mother to the child, or the constancy of the attention she provides that matters profoundly, but the quality of the care that the child receives from the mother, or from both parents, or from a substitute parent. In the more recent considerations of the bearing of maternal employment upon child development, this point is repeatedly stressed and supported by clinical and other evidence.

[8] Harold E. Stearns, ed., *Civilization in the United States* (New York: Harcourt Brace, 1922), p. 336

All this invites speculation about the character of child-mother relationships in the past when fewer mothers worked outside the home, but when industrial homework was far more common than it is now, when part-time work by women was probably far less common that at present, when housework was physically more exacting and time-consuming, and when wives produced within the home many of the goods and services they purchase today. Thus, from one point of view, what may be of special significance in the change in women's work is its shift from within to outside the home, and, the resulting longer periods of continuous *separation* between the mother and child, rather than any major reduction in the *total amount of time* which the mother devotes to child care. It is, of course, easy to forget that what constitutes a full-time job in number of hours worked today would have been regarded as a half-time job in many occupations and industries sixty and seventy years ago.

In any case, if the changes in women's work during the present century constitute a major social transformation—as it seems evident they do—their significance for the children and youth of the nation will not be illuminated solely by more intensive and extensive studies of altered patterns and practices of child care, however important they are. What is required is a series of inquiries into the full range of consequences which presumably flow from having so large a proportion of wives and mothers engaged in employment outside the home. If it be objected that this is merely an invitation to reexamine many facets of American life which are already being actively studied from other vantage points, the simplest and briefest reply is, "Why not?" Each new

vantage point skillfully utilized for research purposes provides fresh insights and information, and there is every
reason to expect that this one would do no less.

At present, all too little of a reliable nature is known
about the implications which the new patterns of women's
employment have for the meaning of work in the society,
for the educational opportunities and experiences of the
young, for the duration of marriage and the incidence of
divorce, for the interpersonal relationships of husbands and
wives both within and outside the family unit, for the parental role and functions of fathers, for family income and
spending, for the availability of free time and the nature of
leisure, for the character and adequacy of welfare policies
and services involving children, and for a host of other subjects.

It was pointed out earlier that an explanation of how the
twentieth-century revolution in women's employment came
about "would require retelling the history of the United
States." It is no less true that an examination of the society's
contemporary life from the viewpoint of employment outside the home by wives and mothers would provide a new
range of understandings of the nation's recent social and
economic history.

CHILDHOOD IN TWENTIETH-CENTURY AMERICA

by ERIC LARRABEE

CHILDHOOD in America is not only admired; it is looked upon as a national asset, somewhat on a par with the Declaration of Independence or the Mississippi River. We like to think of it as a good in itself, and to lament its passing. We hang onto the images of youth that are thought to be traditional—the barefoot boy, the old swimming hole, the sandlot games—though in fact few of us may ever have known them in life. *Tom Sawyer* is a dominant picture of boyhood, just as *Huckleberry Finn* is almost a national epic; and the loss of innocence is a persistent theme in our literature.

So it is for other nations too, and I mention these qualities to describe us rather than set us apart as unique. Yet one can imagine attitudes toward childhood different from ours. Children can be thought of as vessels to be filled, animals to be restrained, plants to be encouraged, or simply as adults in the process of becoming. And though surely children are

Eric Larrabee is Executive Editor of *American Heritage*.

universally loved, the state of being a child is not universally
esteemed. In some societies it may be no more than an inter-
val spent in training for maturity, to be got through as rapidly as possible. The comparison has of course been made—
so often as to be commonplace—between American children
and their European peers, who have been taught to act like
little grown-ups, and are startlingly "well behaved" by contrast.

Childhood in America is also something that adults experience vicariously. It plays a large part in the national diet
of stories and symbols. Children are continuously observed
and recorded in the act of being themselves, and their documented behavior is everywhere available, from the consoling
normalities of Spock and Gesell to the revolutionary defi-
ance of Dennis the Menace. Short stories about children, as
many magazine editors have commented, make up a discon-
certingly large proportion of the manuscripts sent in by fic-
tion writers, since those attracted to emotional nuance so
often find their favorite subjects in the very young or very
old, who are supposed to escape the uninteresting routines
of getting and spending, and live mainly in their senses. But
the place where children are most prominent of all is in
advertising. There they frequently play the role of the ultimate audience, whose approval of a product is spontaneous
and unpurchasable, and therefore greatly to be respected.

They are looked upon as important, however, largely in
adult terms. Though children are increasingly entitled to be
labeled as a "market" in their own right, they do most of
their consuming through adult proxies. Toys are less often

designed to please children than to please adults' ideas of
what children should like, and the father who forces on the
family the electric train he really wants for himself is a
familiar figure in our folklore. "For the children's sake" is
one of the most unanswerable arguments in the conven-
tional repertoire of American conversation; it removes virtually all questions from the realm of debate, particularly
those that involve one's neighborhood or style of life and are
likely to be subject to the worst anxieties. The mass migration to the suburbs of the postwar parental generations has
drawn heavily on this argument, even where it was obvious
that "for the children's sake" actually meant: "In order not
to have to be bothered by the children."

Some of the disillusionment with suburban utopias may
come from the discovery, made by those who fled there in
such high hopes, that suburban children can no longer be
brushed out into the backyard and ignored until mealtime.
The city dilemmas follow close behind and, as each new
community becomes in its turn overcrowded and over-
equipped, the skillful managing of schedules and facilities is
ever more exigently required of the parents. That they are
little more than chauffeurs for their sons and daughters is
another of the current clichés, but it has its somber side: the
half-humorous dismay over problems of family organization
may tend to replace the accepted parental image of a loving
authority—as, to a degree, it already has been replaced—by
that of a manipulative expediter. *Life* magazine has run
several features which encourage this tendency, showing
mothers on the one hand who are overpowered and ex-

hausted by their offspring, and children's parties on the other hand which have been suavely arranged for a minimum of adult wear-and-tear. The assumption, in each case, is that children are a "problem" to their parents.

What seems to be happening here is an invasion of childhood's world by a set of adult demands. First of all we demand to have children—a demand so great as to overturn the predictions of demographers and outrun the resources of adoption agencies—as if they were the natural prerogative, if nothing else, of a prosperous normality. That an adult feels entitled to children, or guilty at not having them, is bound to be a burden on the children themselves, whether they are natural or adopted; and at worst it invites the parents of low humane capacity to treat their charges like part of the expected middle-class furniture, and harass them for being insufficiently decorative and creditable. Among the varieties of modern parent that, as a nonparent, I find least easy to admire are the ones who present their children as adjuncts of their own personalities, and treat some trivial misbehavior as though it were a defect in themselves, thus prolonging and exacerbating a painful and unnecessary embarrassment.

Society uses childhood to initiate its apprentice members, and we need not be surprised that its methods are sometimes harsh. They have to be. But there is a difference—or there ought to be—between the understandable concern of adults over their successors, and the use of children as an outlet for adult tensions and frustrations. Under a system of arbitrary parental administration, in the small-town world where they

could roam at will, children were often able to construct a
semi-independent enclave insulated from adult distractions.
But with the decline of unquestioned adult authority, and
the drawing in of family life to limited quarters, there has
come to be a premium on cooperativeness and "understanding," and with it a weakening of childhood's traditional de-
fenses against its eternal enemy.

Child-training is an expression of culture, just as much as
sonnets or postage stamps, and behavioral scientists of every
stripe have found it a happy hunting ground for evidences
of social change, psychological theory, or national character.
One would expect that a newborn baby, within reasonable
limits, would always be pretty much the same kind of animal; but of course different societies in different ages have
persisted in picturing it quite differently—pictures that are,
in fact, society's changing picture of itself. Nor have we
escaped from this in our time. What may seem to be a
statement of desirable practice with infants can still turn
out, on examination, to be a statement of adult attitudes
toward other adults.

One of the most striking expositions of this idea was made
by Martha Wolfenstein in an article for the *Journal of Social
Issues* in 1951, called "The Emergence of Fun Morality." In
it Miss Wolfenstein compared the various editions—over
the years since 1914, when it was first issued—of the *Infant
Care* booklet published by the Children's Bureau of the
United States Department of Labor. This is a presumptively
neutral and authoritative document—representing, as Miss
Wolfenstein writes, "at any given time a major body of spe-

cialized opinion in the field"—and it has been widely used
(by 1952 over 28,000,000 copies had been distributed). But
the most remarkable thing about it is the manner in which
it changed between 1914 and 1945.

In the 1914 edition the infant is represented as a creature
of strong and dangerous impulses. "The child is described
as 'rebelling fiercely' if these impulses are interfered with,"
Miss Wolfenstein writes. "The impulses 'easily grow beyond
control' and are harmful in the extreme: 'children are sometimes wrecked for life'. . . . The mother must be ceaselessly
vigilant; she must wage a relentless battle against the child's
sinful nature." Quite clearly the writers of this early edition
thought they were stating nothing but the self-evident facts
of infant nature, yet in retrospect it is obvious they were
doing nothing of the kind; they could far better be described
as reflecting the strong, continuing tradition of American
puritanism, which still could view the emerging emotions as
demons to be feared and tamed.

Time was bound to catch up even with the authors of a
government pamphlet, and by twenty years later there had
been drastic revisions in the text. "We find in 1942–45,"
Miss Wolfenstein goes on, "that the baby has been transformed into almost complete harmlessness. The intense and
concentrated impulses of the past have disappeared. Drives
toward erotic pleasure (and also towards domination, which
was stressed in 1929–38) have become weak and incidental.
Instead we find impulses of a much more diffuse and mod-
erate character. The baby is interested in exploring his world
. . . Everything amuses him, nothing is excessively exciting."

In this contrast we can see a change taking place, not in
the nature of babies, but in the climate of opinion about
the nature of impulses. Is it good to do what one likes? asks
Miss Wolfenstein. "The opposition between the pleasant
and the good is deeply grounded in older American morals
(as in many other ascetic moral codes). There are strong
doubts as to whether what is enjoyable is not wicked or
deleterious. In recent years, however, there has been a
marked effort to overcome this dichotomy, to say that what
is pleasant is also good for you. The writers on child training reflect the changing ideas on this issue.

"In the early period there is a clear-cut distinction between what the baby 'needs,' his legitimate requirements,
whatever is essential to his health and well-being, on the one
hand, and what the baby 'wants,' his illegitimate pleasure-
strivings, on the other. This is illustrated, for instance, in the
question of whether to pick up the baby when he cries. In
1914, it was essential to determine whether he really needs
something or whether he only wants something. Crying is
listed as a bad habit. . . . In 1942–45, wants and needs are
explicitly equated. 'A baby sometimes cries because he wants
a little more attention. He probably needs a little extra attention under some circumstances just as he sometimes
needs a little extra food and water. Babies want attention;
they probably need plenty of it.' What the baby wants for
pleasure has thus become as legitimate a demand as what he
needs for his physical well-being and is to be treated in the
same way." Thus was "permissiveness" endorsed, these many
years ago, by the Department of Labor.

The change that chiefly interested Miss Wolfenstein was
a related one in the attitudes toward play. "Where impulses
are dangerous and the good and pleasant are opposed, play
is suspect. Thus in 1914, playing with the baby was regarded
as dangerous; it produced unwholesome pleasure and ruined
the baby's nerves. . . . The mother of 1914 was told: 'The
rule that parents should not play with the baby may seem
hard, but it is without doubt a safe one. A young delicate
and nervous baby needs rest and quiet, and however robust
the child much of the play that is indulged in is more or less
harmful. It is a great pleasure to hear the baby laugh and
crow in apparent delight, but often the means used to produce the laughter, such as tickling, punching, or tossing,
makes him irritable and restless'. . . . The dangerousness of
play is related to that of the ever-present sensual impulses
which must be constantly guarded against."

To this the later editions oppose a completely contrary
view. Play is now connected with the healthy, exploratory
activities of the infant human organism: "A baby needs to
be able to move all parts of his body. He needs to exercise."
Furthermore, this impulse and all like it are now diffused,
and involve both mother and child. The pleasant and the
good are not only identical; they are fused together in a new
combination called "fun," which is obligatory for everyone.
"Mothers are told that 'a mother usually enjoys entering
into her baby's play. Both of them enjoy the little games
that mothers and babies have always played from time immemorial.' [This harking back to time immemorial is a way
of skipping over the more recent past.] 'Daily tasks can be

done with a little play and singing thrown in.' Thus it is now
not adequate for the mother to perform efficiently the routines for her baby; she must also see that these are fun for
both of them. It seems difficult here for anything to become
permissible without becoming compulsory. Play, having
ceased to be wicked, having become harmless and good, now
becomes a new duty."

Previously, in the picture Miss Wolfenstein derives from
these pamphlets, parenthood itself had been a test of moral
strength; there were frequent allusions to the mother's "self-
control" and "unlimited patience." But in the recent period
parenthood is defined as a source of mutual enjoyment to all
concerned, including the father, who had hitherto been
little mentioned. There is a new imperative: "You ought to
enjoy your child"—and there is no place in the new universe
for the parent or child who cannot "enjoy" those tasks
which formerly had been defined as merely necessary. "Fun
has become not only permissible but required."

The moral of Miss Wolfenstein's story is a double one;
not only should we be wary of the new tyrannies which
masquerade under the banner of release from the old, but
we should also cultivate a saving skepticism about the going
theories of child care. They are of their time, no more, no
less, and there may be much in them even now of fashion
and the misconceptions made palatable only through general acceptance. Indeed, the pendulum swings today so rapidly that we may react against a given school of thought
almost before it has a chance to add its characteristic frag-
ment of truth to the communal store. There is already under

way an attack on "progressive" education—and the demand
for a return to the supposed "standards" of the old-fashioned
school—while it is still a question whether we have yet
learned to be anywhere near "free" enough. Compared to
the old, the modern tyrannies have the advantage of being
almost invisible; but they bear down with no less weight on
the emerging unorganized personality.

To take another example from the literature of social science, there is a vividly illuminating article called "The
Middle-Class Male Child and Neurosis," by Arnold W.
Green, which appeared in the *American Sociological Review*
in February 1946. Green takes the position that two of the
frequently accepted "explanations" of mental ill health—
that it originates during childhood in thwarted love, or because of the arbitrary exercise of authority, as in the old-
fashioned home—do not in fact explain one of the common
neuroses of American males. Instead, under the modern
mantle of demonstrative affection and mild rule, Green finds
even greater danger of a child's inner integrity being weak-
ened or violated.

Green begins by describing, as a basis of comparison, the
life of lower-class Polish families in the Massachusetts industrial village in which he himself grew up. Their homes
appear to be brutal and devoid of warmth; the sound of
blows and voices raised in anger issue from them so continuously as to warrant little or no attention. Yet the children do not become neurotic. However harsh the parental
authority, it remains—so Green writes—"in a sense, casual
and external," the parents having neither the means nor the

opportunity to invade the essential core of the child's self. There are likely to be many children, offering many models of possible behavior and yet presenting a united front in rebellion against the older generation's poor English, attachment to the "old country," or lack of sophistication about American ways. The houses are neither clean nor filled with objects of value, so that the child "is spared the endless admonitions which bedevil the middle-class child not to touch this or that."

Under such circumstances, child-training is haphazard and easygoing, "very similar to the training received in many primitive tribes," and it makes a sharp contrast to that of the typical native-white, Protestant, urban, college-educated, middle class. Here the heart of the parental attitude toward children is ambiguous. The father finds that his duties and obligations are increasing, while his rights steadily diminish. The mother, interrupted in a career half-seriously begun, has been thrown into household tasks—even with a plenitude of gadgets—which her training defines as drudgery and encourages her actively to dislike. No matter how deeply loved and desired, children in such families cannot help but seem a psychological and financial drain, a continuously limiting factor on career and social life.

Here the mother, as Green writes, "is her single child's sole companion. Modern 'scientific child care' enforces a constant supervision and diffused worrying over the child's health, eating spinach, and ego-development; this is complicated by the fact that much energy is spent forcing early walking, toilet-training, talking, because in an intensely com-

petitive milieu middle-class parents from the day of birth
on are constantly comparing their own child's development
with that of the neighbor's children. The child must also be
constantly guarded from the danger of contacting various
electrical gadgets and from kicking valuable furniture. The
middle-class child's discovery that the living-room furniture
is more important to his mother than his impulse to crawl
over it unquestionably finds a place in the background of
the etiology of a certain type of neurosis, however absurd it
may appear."

Without companions, tied down to a restricted area, the
child's animal expansiveness and boredom inevitably involve
him in what his culture defines as "trouble": "screaming,
running around the apartment, upsetting daddy's shaving
mug, rending teddy-bear in two, emptying his milk on the
rug to observe what pattern will be formed. This 'trouble' is
all a matter of definition. Similar behavior, in modified form,
would not be interpreted in primitive society as 'trouble,'
and neither would it be by Polish parents in the community
described above."

With the emphasis that the modern period puts on love,
especially within the middle classes, the most effective response to "trouble" on the parents' part is to threaten to
withdraw their love. "The more ambivalent the parents are
toward the child, the more seriously is the 'trouble' he causes
them interpreted. He should not act in such a way because
of the sacrifices they have made on his behalf, and the least
he can do is show his gratitude by 'loving' them in turn, i.e.,
keeping out of 'trouble'. . . . Mamma won't like you if you

don't eat your spinach, or stop dribbling your milk, or get down from that davenport. To the extent that the child's personality has been absorbed, he will be thrown into a panic by this sort of treatment, and develop guilt-feelings to help prevent himself from getting into further trouble. In such a child a disapproving glance may produce more terror than a twenty-minute lashing in little Stanislaus Wojcik."

Later, when the middle-class child begins to emerge into middle-class society, he discovers that his attempts to escape from guilt within the family involve him only in guilt outside it. He is now expected to be purposeful, independent, and competitive. "He is expected to 'do things,' to accomplish, perhaps to lead in some endeavor, like other children. . . . At first he felt guilty only if he failed to love and obey, and his guilt could be assuaged by the propitiation of submission; now, however, the god-monsters will be appeased only by a combination of submission in his role of child-in-family, and assertiveness in his play-group, school-pupil, and other roles enacted outside of home. An integration of these conflicting roles is impossible. . . . He is damned if he does and damned if he doesn't. He is embraced by a psychological Iron Maiden; any lunge forward or backward only impales him more securely on the spikes."

He has been victimized by adults.

Admittedly, these inroads into the child society are made without great calculation or intent. It is rare enough for adults to remember that they once were children, let alone to reconstruct imaginatively their own childlike incomprehension of the adult world. The two universes are opposed,

yet that of the child is continually eroded by the leakage of
its members into maturity, and the veil of forgetfulness that
falls between them and their past. One may view this partial
amnesia as fortunate or unfortunate—certainly it is the latter for novelists, whose childhood is their prime source of
fresh and glistening sense impressions—but in either event,
it is a permanent obstacle to adult interpretation of childhood's major experiences.

To the child, the most evident and annoying fact about
grown-ups is that they do not understand—they do not take
in an event directly, in the fullness of its happening, with
all of its qualities intact. To the child, so much is occurring
for the first time that events come through to the mind
complete, carrying their full load of atmosphere and conno-
tation. He lives immersed in the state of nature which adults
can attain only by a supreme effort, in which no fact is
without value and the mind can consciously apprehend more
dominions and powers than it can find words to describe.
The human brain is a matchless device for screening and
filtering out the messages sent to it by the senses, and converting them into "intelligible"—that is, previously recognized and labeled—patterns. But the penalty of perfecting
it is a narrowing wave-length, like a loud speaker that will
convey only a sodden, restricted band of the total spectrum
of sound.

Just as a dog can hear a whistle pitched above the human
limit of audibility, so a child may "hear" a range of phe-
nomena denied to adults. Having just emerged from the
preverbal culture of infancy, he still retains some of its

capacity for nonverbal intelligence, while for adults what cannot be put in words might just as well not exist. If a house is filled with hate, a child will often know it long before he has learned to explain, even to himself, what his sensations are telling him. And it is this evident disparity between the world as he knows it and the world as officially described that often gives him his extraordinary sense of rightness, of being in tune with the cosmos, regardless of what "they" say. In favorable circumstances, he may even share this conviction with other children.

Shared conviction is a prerequisite of "play," in so far as play is considered as the self-contained ritual by which children exclude other realities than their own. "May I play with Johnny?" Play has a definite starting point and stopping point, a moment when its own terms take hold and a moment when their spell is broken. The material of the drama ("what shall we play?") is unimportant; what matters is the assertion of a superior reality, of being drenched in organized meaning and cleansed—as the adult imagination can be cleansed by art—of the psychic dust and dirt accumulated in the daily round. The fact that play is patronized by adults is high on the child's agenda of dissatisfaction with them; he resents both their intrusion on its sacred precincts and their apparent ignorance of its beguiling and ennobling potentiality.

The idea has by now been thoroughly popularized that primary emotional patterns are set in childhood, yet this period is still only partially credited with its considerable contributions to the world of work and worry. Look, for example, at that most "American" of methods for the accomplishment of tasks: the combat team. What is it but the "gang" of American childhood, recapitulated in adult terms? Characteristically, we break down any organizational situation, no matter how large, to the half-dozen or so of our immediate, face-to-fact colleagues, the manageable unit that temperamentally accords with our earliest memory of a "group." There is always the leader, though he or she may not be the senior, nor assured of tenure; just as there are always the stalwarts, the goof-offs, and the one or two siblings dragged along for the ride. Childhood created it, childhood trains us in it long before we see the inside of a schoolroom, or discover the voluminous duties that organized adulthood is prepared to impose.

The "iron maiden" that Arnold Green describes is in itself not a bad introduction to what Erik H. Erikson has called (in *Childhood and Society*) the "dynamic polarities" of American life: between migratory and sedentary, competitive and cooperative, individualist and conformist, radical and conservative, responsible and cynical, and so on. It must help us to have handled when we were young at least one set of irreconcilable alternatives. As Erikson puts it, "the American, on the whole, lives with two sets of 'truths' . . . [he] must be able to convince himself that the next step is up to him and that no matter where he is staying or going he always has the choice of leaving or turning in the opposite direction if he chooses to do so . . . for the life style (and the family history) of each contains the opposite element as a potential alternative which he wishes to consider his most private and individual decision."

In this the novelists do us a disservice when they persist in treating childhood as the lost abode of a fugitive and an irretrievable innocence. The child, in their hands, has become a kind of twentieth-century equivalent of the eighteenth-century Noble Savage, a repository of our fears and fantasies. The result is a mounting concentration of adult attention—too much attention, and for the wrong reasons—on a time of life that is difficult enough without it. Already adolescence, as a period of fruitful immaturity, is showing signs of disintegration under the massed assault of its anxious elders. Their compulsive concern over such irrelevancies as teen-age delinquency, rock-'n-roll, or steady-dating (so Edgar Z. Friedenberg maintains, in *The Vanishing Adolescent*) has made it increasingly difficult to *be* an adolescent—and, therefore, to grow up. Perhaps, Friedenberg suggests, age is overly interested in youth to the extent that age finds itself uninteresting.

There have been some admirable efforts to visualize and describe the self-contained society of the child, among recent ones the comic strip *Peanuts* or Robert Paul Smith's best seller, *"Where Did You Go?" "Out." "What Did You Do?" "Nothing."* Smith is especially successful in describing the small-town childhood of an earlier generation, with its strong streak of self-reliance and disdain for all other values than its own. Who now knows how to play mumbly-peg, Smith asks? What has become of all the arcane lore that children

faithfully passed on to younger children? Why do they now
have an overabundance of toys and yet are always asking
for "something to do?" Why, indeed? The same question
could be asked of their elders. For even this intelligent evo-
cation of a vanishing way of life bears the mark of our other
motives, our worries about an America that is in so many
senses too prosperous—in short, about ourselves. The members of a new generation deserve at least the chance to develop their own worries. A little inattention might do them
a world of good.

THE HUMAN COMMONWEALTH

by NORMAN COUSINS

EDUCATION for membership in the human community of the twentieth century is not a matter of an expanded syllabus. It goes beyond subject matter into attitudes, into values. It involves a sense of adventure in seeking new truths about man. It has to do with a respect for the inevitability of change and the need for change.

Education does not exist apart from history. It is at its best when it serves history most, when it deals with the needs and changes produced by human experience. In this sense, education today is far more difficult than it has ever been.

History stopped crawling about eighty years ago and began to catapult. The danger so well described by Whitehead—the danger that events might outrun man and leave him a panting and helpless anachronism—is by now much more than a figure of speech. We have leaped centuries ahead in inventing a new world to live in, but as yet we have an inadequate conception of our own part in that world. We have surrounded and confounded ourselves with gaps—gaps

Norman Cousins is Editor of *Saturday Review*.

between revolutionary science and evolutionary thought, between cosmic gadgets and human wisdom, between intellect
and conscience. The clash between knowledge and ethics that
Henry Thomas Buckle foresaw a century ago is now more
than a mere skirmish.

Confronted with this sudden and severe "upset in the
metabolism of history," as Professor Donald H. Andrews
of Johns Hopkins calls it, what is it we expect education to
do? No single answer can possibly have enough elasticity
to be all-inclusive. We expect it to narrow the gap between the individual and society. We expect it to shorten
the distance between individual capacity and collective needs.
We expect it to produce the rounded man. We expect
it to enlarge the ability to think and the capacity for
thought. We expect it to be helpful in creating constructive
attitudes—both on an individual and a group basis. We
expect it to impart basic and essential general knowledge
for rounded living, and basic and essential specialized knowledge for specific careers. We expect it to develop ethical
values. In short, we expect education to furnish the individual with the necessary intellectual, social, moral, and technical clothing for a presentable appearance in the world community.

But yesterday's clothing no longer fits. Is there sufficient
education for vital participation in the world community?
Is there sufficient emphasis on the most important science
of all—the science of interrelationships of knowledge—that
critical area beyond compartmentalization, where knowledge
must be integrated in order to have proper meaning? Is there

sufficient awareness in the individual that this time is unlike any other time in history, that the human race has exhausted its margin for error? Is there enough of a sense of individual responsibility for group decision? Is the individual equipped to appraise the news and to see beyond the news, to see events against a broad historical flow?

These questions are not academic. They are as real as a long walk in the hot sun, as real as a lost pay envelope, as real as any immediate problem that directly affects the welfare of the individual. For we live at a time when the problems of human destiny are no longer philosophical abstractions reserved for posterity but our own special and immediate concern. Ultimate questions have become present imperatives.

These are vaulting responsibilities; the apparatus of education cannot be expected to assume the entire burden. But at least those responsibilities offer something of a yardstick by which education can measure its own part and place in the total picture.

The problem may be complicated and confounded by many insufficiencies, but at least one of them is not an insufficiency of new knowledge. In fact, new knowledge is being generated so rapidly that it can hardly be classified, much less be absorbed. We know virtually everything except what to do with what we know. We are being hurt or threatened not by what we don't know but by what we do know that we can't put to good use. Our facts are even more out of hand than our machines.

How can education make new knowledge obedient to human purposes? Another way of asking this perhaps is: how do we educate for change?

The main business of a rational society is the business of living with change, comprehending it, and, if possible, making it subordinate to the human situation. In a more limited sense, whether the idea of America survives in this world may depend less upon the amount of destructive force we can develop or use than upon our ability to deal with the problem of change in our time.

There is not a single critical situation in the world today that does not involve the challenge of change. It makes little difference whether we are talking about our relations with the rest of the world or our economy or even our hopes. There is a fast-moving current of change that ties all our problems together. They are tied together in the sense that all of them make insistent demands on us: Either we understand the vital problem of change involved in each case or we are left on an historical siding.

To return to our opening theme: There was a time in the life of nations and civilizations when the pace of change was glacial. The problems of the period of the Enlightenment, for example, were at least two hundred years in the making. The effects were spread out over another century or more. The lifeblood of Greece may have run out in large measure during the Peloponnesian Wars, but the causes fed slowly into that conflict and the consequences distributed their hurt over long years. In fact, ours is the first generation in history that has had to absorb the kind of changes that heretofore took thousands of years to produce.

From 1945 to 1960 we have seen change overtake a large part of the body of systematic knowledge. The one event represented by the liberation of atomic energy may have greater significance than any previous utilization of the scientific intelligence of man. The conquest of earth gravity, as represented by the man-made space ship, may have an even more profound effect on philosophy than upon physics. A sudden new perspective bursts upon the mind. The human brain now begins to perceive, however dimly, the meaning of a universe in which the earth and, indeed, the solar system may occupy a position in relationship to the whole no larger than the atom itself is to this planet.

Nothing has been more difficult in the evolution of thought than for man to depart from his view of himself as central in the universe. But now we have to begin to live with the idea that life, life with intelligence, may exist on millions or billions of planets and may even, in many cases, be far superior to our own.

Meanwhile, even as we prepare to take off for other worlds we seem to be doing our level best to get rid of this one. The means now exist and stand primed for instant use—means that can expunge in a few seconds the work and culture of man that required thousands of years to put together piece by piece. No one knows whether it took man a quarter of a million years to evolve into his present being, or a half million years, or two million years. What we do know is that he has now employed his evolved intelligence in the creation of explosives that would put an end to his place on this earth at least.

Whether the explosives go off or whether this planet becomes a safe place for human life depends not on magical solutions but on the ability of man to understand the challenge of change.

If the use of nuclear military force no longer can achieve victory but threatens universal extinction, then it becomes important to understand this change and attempt to devise means that can be effective in enabling us to preserve our freedoms and values and also serve the cause of humankind in general.

If our security today no longer depends on the pursuit of force but on the control of force, then it becomes necessary for this change to be known and acted upon. Tied to this is the need to educate in connections. That is, to educate in our relationships with the rest of the world.

If we are challenged by a powerful ideology, we can recognize that the only time we need fear an ideology is if we lack a great idea of our own—an idea great enough to encompass change, great enough to unify man and set him free, give him reasonable peace, and make the world safe for his diversity.

Education, which is essentially a process of conversion, can deal with the new conversion skills that are now needed to master change. Humans convert beautifully in the fields of science and technology. They can convert the face of nature into a countenance congenial to human life. They can convert sand, stone, and water into gleaming and wondrous towers. They can convert fluids into fabrics. They can convert the invisible atom into an infinity of power. They can convert the rush of water into the whirling fantasy of the dynamo and thence into the magic impulses that banish darkness or turn wheels or carry images and voices over empty space. They can convert air, agitated by the spin of a blade or the thrust of a jet, into the lifting power that enables them to rise from the earth and fly over the mountains and the seas.

But these are not the conversion skills that are now most needed. What is most needed now by man is to apply his conversion skills to those things that are essential for his survival. Of these, the most urgent and overriding need is to convert facts into logic, free will into purpose, conscience into decision. He has to convert historical experience into a design for a sane world. He has to convert the vast processes of education into those ideas that can make this globe safe for the human diversity. And he will have to learn more than he knows now about converting the individual morality into a group ethic.

Our failure to develop these conversion skills has converted us into paupers. The plenty produced by our scientific and physical skills has not relieved the poverty of our purposes. The only thing greater than our power is our insecurity. All our resources and all our wealth are not enough to protect us against the effects of irrational ideas and acts on the world stage. It makes little difference how magnificent are our new buildings or how impressive are our private kingdoms. If no answer is found to war, all men will die poor.

The universe of knowledge, systematic and unsystematic both, is the key to the new conversion process. It can furnish the basic materials that must go into the making of the new purposes and designs. And, quite possibly, it may furnish some of the motive power for the decision behind the effort itself.

Now some people may take the fatalistic view and say it is too late. They may say that man cannot possibly develop the comprehension necessary to deal with change in the modern world, that he will require many centuries before his conversion skills can be developed as they now need to be developed in the cause of human survival.

But there is a larger view of man—one that history is prepared to endorse. This view holds that the great responses already exist inside man and that they need only to be invoked to become manifest. For man is infinitely malleable, infinitely perfectable, infinitely capacious. It is the privilege of all those concerned with education to appeal to these towering possibilities.

By education I am not thinking of schools alone. I am thinking of all those who work on the frontier of ideas. Education begins with ideas. And ideas, if they are big enough, can unfreeze man and make him effective in turning back the largest threat he has ever known.

So far we have been considering the historical mandate in education. We have been considering the fact of change and the challenge of change. We have been considering the general approaches, the attitudes, the values. All these come before syllabus. But syllabus is the point of prime contact with reality in education. In addition to creating an at-

mosphere in which new approaches become clear, we must
define the courses of study, select the textbooks, and draw
up a time-table for getting from here to there.

How, then, do we go about educating the individual for
membership in the human community of the twentieth century? We do this first of all, I believe, by de-provincializing
education. We can rescue education from the notion of a
compartmentalized world, a world in which peoples and
civilizations have been assigned to two big bundles neatly
marked "East" and "West." We can maintain an essential
and proper respect for the legacy of Western civilization,
but we can also recognize that it no longer serves a useful
purpose to talk about the "destiny of Western man" or the
"uniqueness of Western man" or the "prospects of human
civilization."

The central meaning of living history is that human civilization has at last emerged on a single stage. The problem
is to develop a consciousness of this reality and an education
and a philosophy equal to it. Whatever an individual's
pride in belonging to the West or to the East, it now becomes necessary to develop complementary allegiances, affiliations, and sense of connection. A world geographic unit,
to repeat, has created a single arena for the human community. If that community has no sense of itself, if it is lost
in its own anchronisms, then it will never meet its needs.

What is it that justifies the term, "uniqueness of Western
man?" Is it philosophy or literature or political science or
a common yardstick of values? Is it Christianity that defines
the oneness of the West? Is there a magical biological fluid

that circulates through his body, creating a natural kinship
between Europeans and North Americans and South Americans?

First, let us consider the origin and distribution of the
species. A not uncommon error is to confuse anthropology
with philosophy. "Western" man is Greek and Roman, but
he is also German and Scandinavian and English and Portu-
guese and Spanish and Polish and Russian and much more.
If you go back far enough, there is a common stock, of
course, but by going back just a little farther you can also
include the people of Asia and Africa. Does living in Europe
endow a person with a special chemical attraction for anyone who lives in the Americas? And what part of the Americas are you talking about? Canada? Puerto Rico? The United
States? Argentina?

Is there a biological oneness felt between Germans and
French so that neither party can possibly feel for, say, the
Egyptians? And how would you classify a substantial part of
the Mexican population, with Spanish and Negro and Indian
blood flowing together? Are North American Indians to be
considered East or West? They are authentic Americans;
in fact, they once owned the place, but the anthropologists
relate them to Eastern races. When we talk about the destiny of Western man, then, do we include the Indians of
North and South America?

Or perhaps we are thinking of our political heritage. Clas-
sical Greece, in particular. True, Greece was the vital ground
in which the political roots of democratic government were
planted. It was here that the operation of society became

a political science. The concept of constitutional government, separation of powers, limitation of tenure, direct responsibility of officeholders to the people, rights and duties of citizens—in all these respects Greece made a towering contribution to history. When we add to this the Roman science of laws, we have a legacy that is deeply felt, deeply valued, deeply expressed—and rightly so.

Yet even this is not enough to tie the West together and enable us to talk of Western man as a recognizable and complete democratic entity. The history of the West shows far longer periods of monarchy, autocracy, oligarchy, and totalitarianism than it does periods of democratic government. It may be argued that the true lessons of Greece did not begin to be learned for two thousand years; yet even if we confine our scope to recent history we can see that the principal threats to democratic institutions have come from within the West itself. Nazism and Communism, with their nihilism and authoritarianism, are prime disorders within the body of the West. When we think of the citizen as a mighty source of freedom, are we thinking of the individual German under Hitler or the Argentinian under Perón? The fact is that there is neither a political compact in the West nor even a general grouping around commonly accepted values.

If the case for the uniqueness of Western man moves from the political to the intellectual, here again we can pay our debt to the Greek teachers, philosophers, historians, and theoreticians. And we can pay an even greater debt to their disciplined rational intelligence than we do to the actual results of their intellectual labors. If more attention had

been paid to Aristotle as an example of the creative thinker
rather than as the sovereign monarch of all knowledge, perhaps there would have been less intellectual stagnation after
the fall of Rome. As for Plato, it should also be recorded
that many of his ideas on the perfection of man were to
become distorted by numberless self-appointed Platonists,
and that some of these ideas were to be used against man
himself. The fact that versions of neo-Platonism played into
the hands of advocates of a master race and brutalitarians
is not to be held against Plato, of course, but it at least indicates that there is no firm agreement in the West about
what he tried to say or about the practical application of
his thought.

Long before Plato ideas on the need for perfection in man
and his institutions were being voiced and heard in Asia—
especially in China, India, and Persia. The moral code of
Zoroaster, aiming at the triumph of virtue not only over
the material world but over the spiritual world as well, actually helped to fertilize Greek thought. Confucianism is almost synonymous with individual virtue and applied ethics,
and has influenced far more people in the East than have
been influenced by affirmative Platonism in the West. Similarly, it is doubtful whether the logic of Aristotle has made
a more profound impact on any nation than it has upon
Persia, possibly not excluding Greece itself.

The only generalization worth making about East and
West is that there is far more cross-fertilization of ideas than
has been generally acknowledged. A few Western scholars,
such as Gilbert Chinnard, H. G. Creel, John Dewey, Lewis

Mumford, George Sarton, Gilbert Murray, Horace Kallen, Jacques Barzun, Arnold Rowbotham, Bertrand Russell, Ralph Turner, and F. S. C. Northrop, have been concerned with the cross-currents and cross-penetration of ideas that have been associated with geographic East and West. But too little of this has percolated through to the general body of our knowledge of scholarship.

More ought to be said about the mission of the Jesuits to China in the sixteenth and seventeenth centuries, and the impact upon them of Confucianism. They were accused in Europe of having been converted themselves. The favorable accounts of Confucianism they sent back made an important contribution to the development of the French ideas of equality. The Jesuit Le Compte was especially impressed by the absence among the Chinese of hereditary nobility and the absence of caste or other distinctions. The Physiocrat School, so important in the making of the French Revolution, formally acknowledged its great debt to Confucianism, as interpreted by the Jesuits. In turn, Benjamin Franklin and Jefferson acknowledged their debt to the Physiocrats.

It is unimportant whether such influences were primary or secondary. What is important is that neither East nor West held any monopoly, as Jefferson himself pointed out, on the concept of equality. It is interesting, too, to observe the basic similarity in the thinking of Jefferson and Confucius, especially in their concern for the farmer, their cordial disdain for mysticism, their belief in the natural rights of man, their strictures against authoritarianism, their emphasis upon education as a proper function of government, their belief in the full development of the individual's potential, and their unending search for public and private virtue.

Those who are accustomed to making pronouncements about the "mission of Western man" or the "destiny of Western man" will claim that we have so far slighted one fact of mountainous importance: Christianity. Isn't Christian civilization, they will ask, synonymous with Western man? Isn't this what gives Western man the right to think of himself as different and special?

The main trouble with this line of reasoning, of course, is that it assumes that Christianity itself is an entity. Is there general agreement about the meaning of Christ and the teachings of Christ in the West? Is there common acceptance of the same articles of faith? Indeed, are not Christians divided by their beliefs into numberless and occasionally opposing denominations? In a certain sense this is inevitable. So long as they have the capacity for creative interpretation, so long as they can exercise the right of free choice, they will be unable to devise and stay within any single institution or credo. This is natural and right. There is strength in such diversity. But this strength is misapplied if it tries to segregate or compartmentalize humanity into Christians and non-Christians, Eastern and Western man, or make something unique of one man as against another. The province of Christianity is not the ennoblement of Western civilization but the ennoblement of man.

The greatest paradox of all, however, is that the truest expression of Christianity today is to be found, not in the

West, but in the East. In India countless millions of people are living out the ideals of Christ, though they do not call themselves Christians and are unfamiliar with Christian theology. They are the poor and the meek and the merciful and the pure in heart. They regard life as sacred and will not harm it in any of its forms. They practice renunciation. They believe in nonviolence and they worship the memory of a human being who perhaps has come closer to embodying Christianity than anyone in modern history. Interestingly enough, Gandhi's struggle was directed against a Western Christian nation.

Are we to overlook the basic unity of most religions? The code of Hammurabi, the Koran, the Talmud, the Analects, and the Bhagavad-Gita have many of the same fundamental tenets defined in the Sermon on the Mount. What we call the Golden Rule has its parallel expression in almost all other religions. The Islamic faith is as closely related to the Jewish and the Christian faith as the latter two are to each other. It is astonishing to find how little is known about the Islamic religion in otherwise well-educated circles in Europe and the Americas. The extent to which the Mohammedan belief incorporates many of the fundamentals of Judaism and Christianity is overlooked in the frequent references by many Western thinkers to "Judeo-Christian" traditions or civilization. This is properly regarded by the peoples of the Near East as another example of our philosophical and theological provincialism.

"When will the West understand, or try to understand, the East?" asked the Japanese philosopher, Okakura-Kakuze,

more than fifty years ago. "We Asiatics are often appalled by
the curious web of facts and fancies which has been woven
concerning us. We are pictured as living on the perfume
of the lotus, if not on mice and cockroaches. It is either im-
potent fanaticism or else abject voluptuousness. Indian spirit-
uality has been derided as ignorance, Chinese sobriety as
stupidity, Japanese patriotism as the result of fatalism. It has
been said that we are less sensible to pain and wounds on
account of the callousness of our nervous organization!"

The East, of course, is no more a political or cultural or
anthropological entity than is the West, although those who
talk with such careless ease about Western man generally
juxtapose him against Eastern man. What common center
fuses an Afghanistan Moslem with a Filipino Catholic? Or
a Ceylonese Buddist with a Chinese Taoist? The religious
Hindu is as appalled by the paganism of some of his Chinese
neighbors as are the Episcopalians by Jehovah's Witnesses.
Conversely, some Chinese are as baffled by Indian mysticism
and theosophy as many of us are, though it must be recorded that theosophy is a product of the West. And the big-
gest ideological threat in Asia today, Communisn, is not an
Eastern idea but a Western one. What all this adds up to is
not an Eastern entity but a vast complex inside a complex,
with no single unifying thread.

The Asians—1.5 billion of them—happen to share a con-
tinent which is a formal geographic unit only by human
designation and not by divine insistence. To make grooved
and rutted generalizations about these people is to commit
a sin against good scholarship and the human community

at a time when a vast expansion is needed in man's awareness and comprehension of man.

It is astonishing to see how often university conferences in Europe and the Americas on the problems of philosophy or politics in the modern world will allow stock references to Asian peoples and cultures to go unchallenged. One hears about the "disdain for action" or about "lack of systematic thought" or about the "Oriental love of vagueness" or about the "Eastern mentality" or about "typical Eastern mysticism" or about the "propensity for negation."

What is most unfortunate about these remarks is not the polite arrogance which assumes that failure of communication is necessarily the fault of the next fellow, but the unscholarly technique of placing "Eastern" philosophers inside a single academic enclosure. Anyone who has attended a philosophical meeting, whether in Japan or China or Indo-China or India or Pakistan or Turkey, is able to bear witness to the same spread of ideas and approaches, the same display of argumentation over ends and means, the same contrasts of lofty thoughts and plodding trivia that enliven similar meetings in Paris, London, or New York. Imagine, then, a meeting of Filipinos, Japanese, Chinese, Indians, and Pakistani being characterized as though the ideas of only a single philosopher were being examined.

It must also be said that the East has its own provincial philosophers and scholars who lack an adequate background for an understanding of Europe and the Americas and who make the error of dealing in stereotypes and nonexistent entities in writing about the "iniquitous and materialistic

West." Even when they are friendly, they excuse our "rash-
ness" and "impulsiveness" because of our youth. We are "precocious," "mechanistic," "frivolous," "irresponsible," "ambitious," lacking in "perspective," "wisdom," "insight." As
yet, however, Asian scholars have not proclaimed any mis-
sions for Eastern man, nor have they endowed him with
a special claim on human destiny.

What an Eastern philosophical conference has most in
common with a Western philosophical meeting, perhaps,
is an apparent disposition to invest geographical entities with
fixed cultural, ideological, or philosophical components. Thus
it is not unusual to hear Western philosophy criticized as
lacking in sufficient appreciation of the "vital intangibles"
or "elusive but central values." Along with this is the criticism
of "Western thought" as being overly concerned with systems
and techniques and not enough with the domain beyond
man's limited intelligence. This criticism, of course, is merely
the Asian manifestation of a philosophical provincialism
which is not centered in or confined to any single area.

So far as the overriding needs and purposes of man today
are concerned, it is irrelevant to attempt to determine which
set of stereotypes came first or which is more unscholarly or
unfair—that of the West or that of the East. What is important is that a major effort be made by all concerned to
get away from the entity complex. It would be well, perhaps,
if the world of scholarship would enter into a sort of compact on specificity. It should be made clear whether when
we use the term "East" we are thinking of everything from
the Bosporus Straits to the Bering Sea, or whether we have

a specific area or culture in mind. Proper distinctions should be made between Japan and China and India and Pakistan and Indonesia and Siberia and Iran and Syria and Israel. Similarly, when Asian scholars comment on Europe and the Americas it would be helpful to know whether they are thinking primarily of the Balkans or Scandinavia or South America or France or Canada or whatever.

In addition we can liberate ourselves from some of the harmful misconceptions that are so much excess baggage. Consider, for example, the frequent remark mentioned above that the East has a "disdain for action." It is said that it is virtually impossible for Asians to get beyond opinions and into operations. Thus we have heard about Chinese lethargy, Indian passivity, Balinese serenity, and so forth. In the light of recent and current history, that picture can stand some revision. The Civil War in China, stretching over fifteen years, was conspicuous for its lack of lethargy on all sides. Indeed, the missing ingredient appears to have been, not action, but thought. Japanese aggression in concert with the Axis only a few years ago was sharply in contrast to the prevailing conception of an Oriental nation as lacking in drive or dynamics. It is worth noting, incidentally, that industrialization, militarization, mobilization, aggression, and colonization—all of which dominated Japanese life for perhaps a quarter of a century—had previously reached advanced development in the West. So far as India is concerned, the widespread outside impression of an almost universal passivity or impassiveness must be modified in the light of observable facts of life in India for at least fifty years. Passive resistance and noncooperation were the most vital parts of a real *action* program. After independence, intense political activity on the extremes of both left and right—activity from which Indian men of learning and letters sought no immunity or exemption—made India one of the least passive places on the face of the globe. Bali, too, more closely resembles a hotbed of Balkan intrigue than it does the glamorous, languorous land of Covarrubias sketches.

As for the complaint of "Oriental vagueness," I have searched my memory but I can recall nothing more tangible or more vividly conveyed than the needs and hopes of Asian peoples I was able to meet. Most memorable of all was the emphatic detail with which they documented their desire to maintain their freedom and self-respect, and their deep resentment at being regarded as inferior beings fit only to be servants or subjects. Exclusion acts and humiliation by legislation leave them with no vague reaction. If anything, the response is severely normal—almost to the point of being terrifying. True, some Asian writers and philosophers may have cultivated vagueness for vagueness' sake, but it ought not to be difficult to draw up a list of Western writers and philosophers who have some fairly well-developed abilities in that direction themselves.

Then, of course, there is the matter of the "mystical, mysterious, spiritualistic, and occult East." This is becoming more and more of a travel-poster slogan for tourists and less and less a description with any substance behind it. The most populous nation in Asia has had more disdain for the popular conception of mysticism and the occult than perhaps

any country in the world. The intensely practical and down-
to-earth philosophy-religion of Confucius and Lao-tzu has
little scope for higher metaphysics.

Is there nothing, then, that distinguishes the peoples of
Asian countries from the peoples of Europe and America?
Such differences as exist cannot be separated into two large
spatial bundles conveniently tagged "East" and "West."
Many of the distinctions are national rather than continen-
tal, and even here it is important to take into account whatever pluralism may exist inside the nations themselves. In
addition to the pluralisms are the paradoxes. Indeed, not
until the paradoxes are located and defined does the essential
nature of a culture begin to reveal itself. The finest observers,
historians, and anthropologists have all been paradox hunters.
Hunting and comprehending paradoxes is infinitely more
challenging and rewarding than the pursuit of incredible
entities.

We may live in the two worlds of "East" and "West,"
but we have only one planet to do it on. As L. L. Whyte has
written in *The Next Development in Man*, the separation of
East and West is over, and a new history opens rich in
quality and majestic in scale.

Our courses of study, therefore, should be directed to the
entire human arena in today's world, and, more particularly,
to the human situation. They may not be able to embrace
the whole of comparative cultures, but they can at least
develop the grand approaches and an acquaintance with the
essentials. They can also deal with the nature of the contact

points among contemporary cultures. They can help prepare the individual for direct experience in those cultures. They can attempt to deal with the problem of working relationships. They can educate in common problems.

Language studies represent a wide field for expansion—both in terms of early availability and teaching techniques. Advanced school systems are now considering the feasibility of foreign languages in the lowest grades of elementary schools. We can go beyond that. We can utilize the nursery school and thus take advantage of the most responsive period for natural education in languages that an individual can experience. We can use the earliest building blocks of the education process. Tomorrow's well-educated American will be not merely bi-lingual but tri-lingual. In addition to English and French or Russian or German or Italian or Spanish, he will have proficiency in Hindi or Urdu or Chinese or Japanese or several others. He will see no weakening of his loyalty to his own country in the development of a loyalty to the human commonwealth. His awareness of his place in the human family will not run counter to his pride in the history and achievements of his nation. The widening of allegiances, in fact, is a mark of human evolution.

Most of all, of course, the well-educated man in the human community will be able to see a direct connection, not solely between himself and his society at its largest, but between his awareness of the needs of that society and his effective reach in helping to meet them.

SUGGESTED READING

THE OLD GENERATION AND THE NEW by NELSON N. FOOTE

Carr, Edward Hallett. *The New Society*. London, Macmillan, 1951.
Erikson, Eric H. *Childhood and Society*. New York, Norton, 1950.
Galbraith, John Kenneth. *The Affluent Society*. New York, Houghton, 1958.
Mannheim, Karl. "The Problem of Generations," in *Essays on the Sociology of Knowledge*. Oxford, Oxford University Press, 1952.
Riesman, David, Nathan Glazer, and Reuel Denney. *The Lonely Crowd*. New Haven, Yale University Press, 1950.
Stevenson, Robert Louis. *Virginibus Puerisque*. 1881.

RURAL YOUTH by JOHN H. KOLB

Biddle, William W. *The Cultivation of Community Leaders*. New York, Harper, 1953.
Hollingshead, August. *Elmtown's Youth*. New York, Wiley, 1949.
Loomis, C. P. and J. A. Beegle. *Rural Social Systems and Adult Education*. New York, Prentice-Hall, 1954.
Sanders, Irwin T. *The Community: An Introduction to a Social System*. New York, Ronald Press, 1958.
———. *Making Good Communities Better*. Revised ed. Lexington, Ky., University of Kentucky Press, 1952.

NEGRO YOUTH IN THE SOUTH by LEWIS W. JONES

Davis, Allison and John Dollard. *Children of Bondage: The Personality and Development of Negro Youth in the Urban South.* Washington, D.C., American Council on Education, American Youth Commission Studies, 1940.
Davis, Allison, Burleigh B. Gardner, and Mary R. Gardner. *Deep South: A Social Anthropological Study of Caste and Class.* Chicago, Chicago University Press, 1941.
Dollard, John. *Caste and Class in a Southern Town.* New Haven, Yale University Press, 1937.
Frazier, E. Franklin. *Negro Youth at the Crossways: Their Personality Development in the Middle States.* Washington, D.C., American Council on Education, American Youth Commission Studies, 1940.
Myrdal, Gunnar. *An American Dilemma.* New York, Harper, 1944.
Warner, W. Lloyd, Buford H. Junker, and Walter A. Adams. *Color and Human Nature: Negro Personality Development in a Northern City.* Washington, D.C., American Council on Education, American Youth Commission Studies, 1940.

SPANISH-SPEAKING CHILDREN by JOHN H. BURMA

Burma, John H. *Spanish-Speaking Groups in the United States.* Durham, Duke University Press, 1954.
Griffith, Beatrice. *American Me.* Boston, Houghton-Mifflin, 1948.
McWilliams, Carey. *North from Mexico.* New York, Lippincott, 1949.
Mills, C. W., C. Senior, and R. K. Goldsen. *The Puerto Rican Journey.* New York, Harper, 1950.
Padilla, Elena. *Up From Puerto Rico.* New York, Columbia University Press, 1958.
Tuck, Ruth. *Not with the Fish.* New York, Harcourt Brace, 1946.
Welfare Council of Metropolitan Chicago. *Institute on Cultural Patterns of Newcomers.* Chicago, 1957.

JUVENILE DELINQUENCY by ROBERT M. MAC IVER

Aichorn, August. *Wayward Youth*. New York, Meridian Books, 1955.

Bloch, Herbert A. and Frank T. Flynn. *Delinquency: The Juvenile Offender in America Today*. New York, Random House, 1950.

Cohen, Albert K. *The Culture of the Gang*. Glencoe, Ill., Free Press, 1955.

Healy, William and Augusta Bronner. *New Light on Delinquency and Its Treatment*. New Haven, Yale University Press, 1936, 1950.

Robison, Sophia M. *Juvenile Delinquency: Its Nature and Control*. New York, Holt, 1960.

FRONTIERS IN VOLUNTARY WELFARE SERVICES by ELIZABETH WICKENDEN

Boy Scouts of America. *Study of Adolescent Boys*. New Brunswick, N.J., 1956.

Child Welfare League of America. *A Statement of Principles and Policies on Administration of Voluntary and Public Child Welfare Agencies*. New York, 1958.

Coyle, Grace L. *Group Work and American Youth*. New York, Harper, 1948.

Fredericksen, Hazel. *The Child and His Welfare*. San Francisco, Freeman, 1957.

Girl Scouts of America. *Study of the Adolescent Girl*. Part I. New York, 1958.

Gordon, Henrietta L. *Casework Services for Children: Principles and Practices*. Boston, Houghton-Mifflin, 1956.

National Association of Social Work. *Social Work Year Book*. New York.

THE GOVERNMENT'S ROLE IN CHILD AND FAMILY WELFARE by EVELINE M. BURNS

Blackwell, Gordon W. and Raymond F. Gould. *Future Citizens*

All. Chicago, American Public Welfare Association, 1952.
Hill, Esther P. "Is Foster Care the Answer?" in *Public Welfare* (April, 1957).
Housing and Home Finance Agency. *Children and Youth in an Urban Environment*. Washington, D.C., 1959.
United Nations. *Economic Measures in Favor of the Family*. New York, Columbia University Press, 1952.

WORK, WOMEN, AND CHILDREN by HENRY DAVID

Gross, Irma H., ed. *Potentialities of Women in the Middle Years*. East Lansing, Michigan State University Press, 1956.
Myrdal, Alva and Viola Klein. *Women's Two Roles: Home and Work*. London, Routledge and Keegan Paul, 1956.
National Manpower Council. *Womanpower*. New York, Columbia University Press, 1957.
———. *Work in the Lives of Married Women*. New York, Columbia University Press, 1958.
Women's Bureau. *1958 Handbook on Women Workers*, Bulletin 266. Washington, D.C., Government Printing Office, 1958.

CHILDHOOD IN TWENTIETH-CENTURY AMERICA by
ERIC LARRABEE

Erikson, Erik H. *Childhood and Society*. New York, Norton, 1950.
Friedenberg, Edgar Z. *The Vanishing Adolescent*. New York, Beacon Press, 1959.
Liberman, Sally. *A Child's Guide to a Parent's Mind*. New York, Schuman, 1951.
Riesman, David, Nathan Glazer, and Reuel Denney. *The Lonely Crowd*. New Haven, Yale University Press, 1950.
Smith, Robert Paul. *"Where Did You Go?" "Out." "What Did You Do?" "Nothing."* New York, Norton, 1957.